CROSS POINTS

The Poetic Diary of Ms. Tabu

by Ms. Tabu

For Greg -
Sending Love & Light
for your Journey!
Ms. Tabu

For information regarding permission, purchasing additional copies of this publication, or booking Ms. Tabu for your next event, e-mail BookingMsTabu@gmail.com.

First Edition by Mic2Soul Publishing, May 2015

Front cover photograph: Ajani Housen

Author photograph: Robert Cooper

Book cover design: LLPix Designs

Interior design: BZ Hercules

ISBN-13: 978-0-9861728-0-9 (Paperback Edition)
ISBN-13: 978-0-9861728-1-6 (Kindle Edition)

Printed in the United States of America
2 0 1 5 9 0 2 8 9 8

This book is printed on acid-free paper.

ACKNOWLEDGEMENTS

This is more than just my first published book of poetry; this is my poetic diary, way past due, yet right on God's time. There are so many of you who have supported my artistry along the way. You've shown up to see me perform live and host poetry shows. You've taken the time to share when you were touched by something I wrote. You've consistently inquired about when I would release a book, which motivated me to make this happen. You've humbled me in a way that made me realize that this is so much bigger than I am. Through my hardships and greatest downfalls, you've been there. For that, I thank you.

I'm not only taking a leap of faith, I'm wearing my heart on my sleeve. For the first time in my life, I'm being completely transparent, which is both terrifying and refreshing all at once. These are some of the milestones I've personally crossed through to reach my salvation. By sharing these words I've written throughout my life, I pray for someone else to be inspired by the poems that have helped me work through some of my most challenging experiences. It is my hope that this book will encourage a journey of healing and spiritual awakening for others.

CONTENTS

Every woman has a past…
to leave behind

SURVIVOR

It Was You

Who made me scared to walk in parking lots alone?
Looking behind me for a stalker's shadow
It wasn't the stranger in the dark alleyway
It didn't happen the way that they say
It wasn't like the Lifetime Movie Network
I never learned it at school or in the church
You didn't fit the profile of how he would look
Tall, white, and muscular you were
with a snake charm venomously charged
You always pet named us sweetheart
until we were lured, into coils of a deceiver
Don't pretend you don't remember
our screaming faces
while fallen prey to a serial rapist
Don't you say I didn't say it
like my cries to stop you never heard

I was best friends with your sister
and didn't have the heart
to tell her when she told me
about them all
The girls you'd done it to before
and after me
The lifelong problem you've had
remorselessly
Preying on victims repeatedly
The second time was worse
Yes, I remember your words
You said you wanted to make love to me
knowing you'd raped me once already
You knew I'd blamed myself
after you acted like I was crazy
to be hysterical from
unanswered calls for help
and here you were again to
come back for seconds
I can never express the pain I was in
begging you to stop while
you were achieving world rapist records
of how long you could rape me
when your sister was downstairs
sleeping next to some guy
as I was in her bedroom being
violently victimized

Pressed your hands against my mouth
and I could barely gasp for air
as my bloody murder screams
were lost under your body
crushing into me
I never knew making love
could be forcefully

What exactly were you making love to?
Tell me was Satan sitting in the room
with a cigar lit as he applauded you
telling you to go faster, deeper
assuring you nobody would believe her
as you committed blasphemy on my flesh
I died in the heat of a rapist passionate
Skilled at stealing souls
Accused constantly, but somehow
nobody ever knows
You made a liar of me
until finally another victim came forward
and the police wanted me
But I was more than just a file
to benefit the case

I'm a breathing woman
with a survivor's face
and the power that
made you plead guilty
when you knew you'd lose
if that deal wasn't made
How quickly 'innocent' changed
But my testimony is being heard
to this very day
and I hope that every time
you think about the girls you've raped
that you are haunted by my eyes
smudged mascara, streamed with tears
as you're daunted by the moment
over and over again for years
Convicted for your sins
whether in or out of prison
Well that's what you get
for messing with one of God's children

So get used to the feeling
because you know the truth
that the man raping me those nights,
it was you.

Rapist Until Proven Innocent

Rapist until proven innocent!
I'm sorry,
but his finger prints left behind in my system
created a criminal intent way of thinking
Don't you get it???
I can't get close to you
when I travel distances on autopilot
just to escape
Escape the possibilities
and the responsibility
of having to weigh
the probability
that you might be
made from the same genes
that became his mutated DNA
How do I know
what runs through your veins
Through his it was...
snakes, demons, and clowns
Monsters aren't in closets
but in beds of girls like me who slept sound
So we thought, until this disturbance
went bump in the night
Hanging our spirits like heavy curtains
that lost their flow in those eyes

Eyes like chainsaws masked behind toxic pupils
He cut me in half as I died at my own funeral
The me I used to be lied upon my corpse of a body
like a white rose thrown just before the burial
when the dirt has been dug out already
and knotted throats begin to let go
as it hurts to swallow
from the pain that's choked
Funny how that pain took years to clear

But that was nothing compared to
the repetitious stitching I had to do
to make myself whole again
every morning in time for school
The hallways felt empty
with crowds full of people
but somehow it seemed like
everyone knew
the shame he'd woven into
parts of me I never knew existed
or maybe it all just seemed different
now that I was stripped like a paper doll
Left with all of the pieces
but never knowing how
I was supposed to put me together

So I hated myself
for everything I couldn't be
For the way I couldn't fit
into the skin of me
For the way I couldn't even
let my own father look at me
because every single man became you
and so no wonder I never wound up with
the right one when they were all the same
in my warped, twisted brain
I tried to remember
what it was like being sane
What the scent of flowers was like
before my senses were icy chains
wrapping around my sense of reality
No longer was I
merely a victim of rape
but I was rape

Every time I looked in the mirror,
I couldn't see my face
I prayed the image would
get clearer, one day
that I'd be able to apply lip gloss
without hearing the echoes
of whom I used to be, from afar
that I'd be able to have intimacy
with somebody who could love my scars
Now finally I am the epitome
of freedom, fighting for the cause
and I think I like this me better
than the me I was before after all.

Never Enough Soap

There was never enough soap
to scrub them off of my skin
Never enough body wash
to repent me of their sins
The hot water always ran out too soon
Shivering in tears as my skin pruned
But somehow I was convinced
that I could be cleaned of you
by the fifth lather through
Only to find myself rinsing off residue
But the filthy feeling kept growing
as soap became the obsessive compulsion
behind shower doors where no one could see
I devoured into the floor wishing
somebody could love me
because clearly, soap wasn't working
when I was still hurting
See, Dove couldn't birth me new wings
and bath bubbles didn't nurture me to healing
from the history of abuse I'd been through
Dirty secrets that I couldn't even admit myself to
But they still branded curses to my flesh
Still felt the sting, and the worthlessness
Some of them I never faced
until the process of deliverance
Bars of soap no longer
were a way to escape
what these men did
before and after what I consider
the most violent and defining experience
of being unquestionably raped
during the attempts that were a great success
depending on whose perspective
Because from mine, his achievements were
a sacrifice of my freedom

But surely, he doesn't receive all of the credit
for the molesters and the manipulators
For the locked up memories that messed with my head
but I didn't quite know what to make of them
All I knew was that I was dirty, ashamed
Used, a tangled rose with weeds round' my roots
depriving me of the freewill
to live, to choose, to love, to breathe
to drink, I felt... so thirsty
like water vapors me
before it could quench my needs
They'd washed away my innocence
and soap became my purity
as I watched an angel
slip from my hands, down the drain
I knew I would never be the same again
I had fallen from the heaven I once knew within
as the drain sold my soul to compensate for their sins
then it told me I had no choice but to 'like' it.

No More Nightmares

For many years horrible things plagued my dreams
as my subconscious pulled them from my reality
Every single night, men were chasing me
trying to kidnap me, rape me, and abuse me
until one night when I
murdered all of these demons in my sleep
and never again did I have to worry
that my peace would be disturbed by
tragedies of the past
or the men who have hurt me
would haunt me like that
No more waking up in pools of sweat
trying to catch my breath
But the one thing that always stood out
was that in every nightmare, I'd survived
None of these men could get me
I fought for my life every time
I had the will in me to escape
and that didn't change
no matter how many times I'd awake
I knew no matter what I'd always be okay
When need be, I'd always be brave
and while these men may still walk this earth
God had freed me of this nightly curse
Cleansed me of reliving the burns
Brought me out of the fire
where my spirit still lingered
See sometimes, bad dreams
are nothing more than bad dreams
But sometimes they are memories
used to attack you by the enemy
No longer could he pester me
Mess with me, mentally
Must I add that I've no shame

for the blood shed
while in the REM phase
in order for me to be sane
Some people don't deserve to live...
inside of our brains
So no, I don't feel guilty
for breaking free from the chains
and besides, they were just nightmares
At least, that's what they say.

TOXIC

The Other, Other Woman

Never thought the day would come
I'd have to see you standing next to her
Knowing I've got to bite my tongue
What could I possibly say to change the hurt?
Already told you that I love you
Already gave my heart to you
Already sold a little soul every time I'd lay with you
Already served you the cake on a silver platter
one too many nights, leaving my emotions battered
Already realized I never mattered
the day I found out the hard way I was
the other, other woman
I was just part of the pattern
There's no such thing as
being a man's only other woman

If he's fooling on her with you,
there's always another woman
Trust me when I tell you sisters
And believe me when I tell you brother
When you see me with another lover
Don't act like you didn't think the day would come
when I'd finally find the strength to move on
I've sacrificed one too many of my beliefs
just to be another mistress in your sheets
I've done things with you I'd kill for
if a man did to me
I've played the home girl role
to keep your darkness out of reach
I've already spent too many days playing house
Even coming out of pocket due to your zero balance
Wish I never gave in
Should have left when I had the chance to go
Should have never fallen in love with a ho
There's nothing anyone can tell me right now
because I already know
I must hold myself accountable in order to grow.

Broken, but Still Breathing

He told you that you were nothing
Every argument seemed to be about
all the things that you do wrong
Your faults, your flaws
You are always the cause
the reason it starts
And then, he told you he loved you
as he climbed between your sheets
He knew just the way to numb you
from all the pain he brings
His sweet nothings mean nothing
but they still sound so sweet
They make do for those
tender moments
when you pretend
he's the man you met
in the beginning
But then it is finished
so there you lay
Broken, but still breathing
Hopeless, but heart beating
Counting all the reasons
why you know you should leave him.

Desert Empress

You left me here in the desert with no cactus in sight
Lungs dry, skin burnt through the epidermis layers
You didn't know if I'd survive but you didn't consider
just like a cactus I've adapted to these climates
Shriveling up those roots that were attached to you
like the soil during this manmade drought
Thirsty for the first hint of rain
My new roots are ready
to shoot out just below these grounds
These sands, and these snakes cannot take
all the water I've conserved
Although some evaporates
every time I open up my pores, just to breathe
Walking away with your canteen
like you think you've gotten all of me
But you couldn't take away these seeds
For each fruit I reproduce from my exotic flowers
bear thousands from which I manifest
my knowledge into wisdom on this quest
And although it may take two years
just to birth these legends of me
Believe me, I will survive out here
You can eat me
and you can drink me
and leave me empty
But I don't need a man to replenish me
I don't even need a man to protect me
See my spines growing in thicker clusters
I feel my sap becoming more potent
and poisonous with each minute
You don't see the ancient temple I live in
because it isn't visible to men with blind hearts
and legs that move with their eyes
instead of with what they feel
So you tortured me, forcing me to hear

screeching silence in my ear drums
Talking, but saying nothing
Your lies make me deaf!
I don't have to talk to say something
I don't even need sign language
I stand before these desert winds
and I know the spirits hear it
They hear me sing myself to sleep
A meditation so deep that my life
has become a dream
I'm living each piece
I feel the puzzle formatting like
tectonic plates making alliance for the first time
The war wasn't worth it anymore
So much has been lost by going against nature
God take me, you can destroy me
if it means they can't rape me
of my rights to be free
Make it all fall apart if you can show me
a better way to build these pyramids
beneath my mental spring of eternity
A sanctuary place I long to be
while my hypodermic layer peels away
Father save me from this pain
Remind me again that I am
your child from your kingdom
Deem me worthy of this crown again
Please shame and save these men
and the women who follow them
I'd rather die than give in to being taken
and placed in the society they live in
I will never be potted
even if it means that I will never be wanted
Prepare for me a king who deserves this red carpet
Show him the way to walk it

where he will find me on my throne
surrounded by desert roses
that recite my poems
in a voice sweeter than the strings
of a Bohemian harp
Stronger than the rattle snakes scales that peel off
Let them be the muscle of my heart
Let him hear my voice and fall
beneath the sunsets palm
Carry him to me when his conscious is lost
Let him use your spirit like a camel's back
Give me the key to make him restore
A key that will fit in no other lock
A key that thieves cannot copy
and temptresses cannot mock
Plant that key between the walls
of that sacred spot
He will enter in the name of God
Live and die for your cause
Resurrect our spirits when you take us
Bring us the heavens
Bring us the stars
Bring home the empress of this desert
I've shown you survival
Now show me my worth
I'm done with the belly dance recital
I don't need these skirts
I don't want just the show anymore
and the external glamour
I don't want to be a broken ballerina
dancing on quicksand
While I have been the desert empress
my journey here, must be finished.

Don't Think

Don't think you're the only one
who's ever hurt me before!
Don't believe nobody
has ever hurt me much more
It's not all it seems
It's just the present moment being mourned
So please don't let the flattery distort, me moving forth
You seem to think its all fun, a vindictive game
You don't realize I'm serious, envisioned me playing
and all of these parrots want a part in the vain
I couldn't care less about what they are saying
cause' this is my heart, not a parade
I don't care whose marching along your drummer today
Don't you think for a minute I'm entertained!
Never found the pain as amusement
It doesn't take bruises to make it abusive
Of all the perfect moments ruined,
apologies never were your style
Yet you said a man should never steal my smile
So I take those words with a grain of salt
Occasionally check my missed call log
Slowly, surely losing interest in picking up to talk at all
I'd rather pretend this love were all fraud
and let you go around claiming action, not cause
while true colors bleed through the applause
Don't have to pull your number, leave that one to God
Don't you think you're in the position to ever count my loss
when I'm the one who has distanced off this far
Don't believe I'm not capable of breaking your heart
Just because the poison comes sweet, doesn't mean it wears off
Bet you thought you'd never taste it, yet you gave it
Bet you thought it was enough to keep me wasted
Didn't see all the times I spit it out, behind your back
Would have been the proper dosage if you kept tabs
when you thought you were the only one

who’s ever hurt me before!
It's just like going back to prison
Different crime, same war
In this case here love's been committed
But, no more.

Flowers

She could never trust a man who gave her flowers
because the last man gave her many... flowers
during the honeymoon phase
of the cycle she called love
Granting him unconditional full immunity
from facing the consequences of his actions
which should have been her leaving him
but she stayed
And the longer she was in it,
the more she grew to hate flowers
as she knew what they were symbolic of
The temporary, guiltless, in-genuine apologies
to make it all better until the next time
Somehow he always found a way to blame her
even when he said sorry as though, something she did
were the reason for this, cause and effect
Sorry in his mind, didn't mean he was wrong
It was simply what he had to say
for her to stick around through his abuse
and for her to submit
to letting him climb on top of her
despite the resentment
that sealed the pain within
And then everything
would be wonderful for some weeks
until her humanity peeked through
and she couldn't master
walking on eggshells any longer
Speaking her mind, venting her feelings
Having something to say, how dare she!
And he was smart,
because he abused her deeply
but the evidence of such lived within her
rather than on her skin for the world to see
He beat her...

heart, mind, and spirit instead
The physical forms occurred rarely
so who would ever believe her story
All they would ever see is such a sweet guy
buying her flowers, how lucky she was
but they didn't know
that every time he bought her flowers
a piece of her had died
So now any man who buys her flowers
she deems the abusive type
Don't try to change her mind
She'd rather be wrong and free
then risk being right and fall victim
to the man you might be.

Dear Beloved

I hated you for the first time yesterday
Not to say you never gave me a reason before,
but that the love I feel has begun to harden like cement
to protect those open wounds where you pour your salt
No wonder I'm stinging in my chest!
See I thought flowers were
meant to be nurtured in their natural state
I've never been fond of picking them
just to watch them die
Putting them in a vase, leaving them deprived
There isn't enough sunlight here!
And you can't over flood my wilted petals,
every now and then
with the expectation
for the roots to grow again
Well I've been sitting by this window,
on this shelf for too long
You say I'm so beautiful whenever I look strong
Sketching me in admiration, of my physical
But then you neglect my internal needs again
and it's visible
Is this some kind of power trip,
to bring and take life at the same time?
Already dehydrated, by the time you make me cry
Holding in those tears was my lifeline
Now I've run dry
I have nothing left to give you!
I'm as pitiful as you predicted I'd be
the day you took me for yourself
When did you ever care about
the feelings that I've felt?
If you were an Empath,
you'd be jumping out that window by now.
I've been too strong, should have let the petals fall
until there was nothing there for you to want

Should have been a slave for what I believed in
just to get my freedom.
I'd rather die for me, then live for you
Every time I wouldn't bend the way you want me to
suddenly I'm fair game for abuse
then I'm to blame for fighting back
How dare I defend myself in this glass!
Every time you saw it begin to crack
You took my kindness for weakness
to selfishly extract purity from my existence
Now it's hard to tell the victim
from the one who has imprisoned
But I'd rather hate you and have the strength to go,
then love you and play the same old game, it don't change
So I hated you for the first time yesterday,
loved myself enough to leave
Broken wings like torn leaves,
but now I've evolved and grown thorns
For as long as you don't want to touch me,
you can't hurt me anymore.

Stronger

You make me laugh the kind of laugh like,
"Well isn't he pathetic!"
I know you would think by now I'd hate you
But I think what pisses you off the most
is that I still have it in me to say
I pray for you, brother
You feel the positive energy radiating off of my body
whenever we are within the same vicinity
and it makes you angry
My love makes your blood boil.
You thought you could take me from God's given soil
where my roots grew since birth
You thought that the rumors you spread
would cause me to feel so much hurt, that I gave up
But I didn't, I gave more
I delved deeper into my passion than ever before.
I started a revolution, a movement
Expanded my careers horizons, to the extent where
even the sky isn't the limit
I'm one thousand times more ambitious
Every time somebody comes and tells me you're at it again
You can't emotionally abuse me in a relationship anymore
so now you want to do it from a distance
As I look at the month we are already in,
I say to myself again, "How pathetic!"
Five months since I left him
He's done everything to break me
just because he is too coward
to admit he loves me
Too coward to realize
that the only thing he should say is sorry
Too coward, to get over me, move on
This wounded deer is wounded no more
You thought I was your piece of meat,
but my limbs have been reborn

I found it in me to walk away from you
when I was addicted to the abuse
Hooked on you like crack
because this was the only treatment I knew
not to mention I was mentally and emotionally
reliving rape when I met you
Having to testify against him all of these years later
when another victim came forward
and you, pretended to be a guidance
when I was searching for some kind of answer
But it was all game, and I was played over and over,
until I was the same girl
who didn't love herself back then
as if I was her all over again
and you were just like the psychopath
I was in a relationship with, all those years ago
A perfect parallel reflection like
traveling back into time while still being right here
I walked through your hell, burned through your fire,
and every night I cried tears
Your own friends warned me about your ways
but maybe by then it was a little too late
I was already in so deep, self-esteem stolen from me
all part of the plan, just to keep me there,
scammed of who I am
And then I still found courage to leave the lion's den
knowing he would attack me and seek revenge
But my escape was so worth it,
no matter what snakes he has
lurking, watching on me,
reporting back to him what they see,
so he can get me when I'm weak
but that is when God is most protecting me
Just consider yourself Satan's failure
and go back to class

See my skin won't go any shade paler
no matter how you act
I won't flinch, I won't cry,
I won't show embarrassment or loss of pride
I won't sweat, I won't bend, I won't break
I won't get a single future wrinkle in my face
from the countless ways you've disgraced,
your own place, on this earth's surface
I won't say I'm a saint, and I'm sure not perfect
but one thing I can say is that I don't go around hurting
people who don't deserve it, or hurting people at all
like I told you before, I pray for you brother
And oh, trust me, if I wasn't a woman of God,
I would call up a brother who would slay you, my brother
But I refuse to threaten you
I refuse to stoop down just to get to you
I need not spread rumors about you,
but I will tell the truth
Meanwhile, you've infected the scene
with lies about me for all of these months
and yet, my real brothers and sisters
still love me because they know what's up
They know all of these things you say,
they just don't add up
Don't take no mathematician to know
I'm a woman manifesting queen visions
not some whore you try to have them mistake me for
Not some liar selling stories, brother
That's your character
Projecting your own reflection
on someone else is one of the oldest
Devil's tricks in the book
You may have gotten to some of them
but you just relieved me of
knowing who my true friends were

Oh, but I pray for them too
Falling for a manipulator like you
Shoot, I pray for anybody who ever
crosses paths with you
I pray that the infestation of negative energy
doesn't poison their thoughts
I remember the way it felt,
the first days you were gone
when I couldn't take it no more
Like rays of light bursting back into me,
so bright that strangers were driven to me
and they didn't even know why
like an angel had come inside of me, just so I could fly
knowing that my vessel was still strung out
on the high of being low
still capable, of relapsing back into that black hole
but she wrapped me tightly with her halo
so I could not only see the light, but I could be the light
You can't look at me because I make you blind with a shine
that has become mine or maybe it always was
and I just needed to face your ugly
so I could see my beautiful
I regret nothing, in fact I'm thankful
I'm thankful for the emotional roller coaster
that controlled me for that year
I'm thankful that you are the last from the slew of men
who have put me through imprisoning situations
I'm thankful that it ended here
I remember when I told you
butterflies don't belong trapped in jars
and your reply was we are easy to catch
I guess you never thought I'd break the chains
when you had my head in a place that wasn't sane
Since then, all of my feelings,
even resentment have been erased

No wonder you are so determined to make me feel hate
because that'd be better than the fact I feel nothing for you
But no matter what you do, I will still pray for you
I have every single reason in the world
to want to kill you but that I won't do
Because I love me more than hating you would be worth
and I'm stronger than before so I thank you for this power
as the Lord continues to shower me
with reward right before your eyes
It is no wonder I'm the woman, you continue to despise
Because I am authorized to be everything you say I'm not
While you're just another demon I've exorcised
on my travels to the top.

Satanic Puppetry

When I realized what you really did to me
How you betrayed my temple from the beginning
How you tranquilized my free will by injecting
some kind of generic version of 'guidance'
into my veins, cut and laced with the blood of
a devil's pilot, crashing into my pain
landing there, just to suck on my open flesh
I have learned vampires come in many disguises
Did you ever know a man who hypnotizes
you to excuse his sin due to biases
such as, "I love him"?
Did you ever know a man who
pretends he's, 'women righteous'
yet is the same man,
draining women of their life bliss?
A man who can turn you off like a light switch
climb upon you and convince you to like it
Did you ever lay there and give in
when you wanted to fight it?
because after hours of hoaxing,
'love' seemed a
good enough reason to be violated
Did you ever think it was love
when you truly felt hatred?
Funny how the past can come knocking
when you least expect it
forcing you to relive something
to the point where you manifest it
and now becomes then
Back in the same abusive situation
you were in back then
after the one who stole your innocence
Mistaking your worst enemy for your best friend
Piranhas for lovers, on some Lauryn,
"Those who pretend to be brothers,"

and I thought he was closest to me
I never knew what a real man was supposed to be
I had my list of things I wanted
but knowing it and living it, are very different
How can you come with a checklist
if you aren't even checking those things for yourself?
How can you be expecting to meet a real man
if you aren't being real to that which you felt?
No matter who stripped you of your right to choose
through what was supposed to be your youth
Understand there is no more excuse
to allow men to release their baggage on you
as if you are responsible for the misery
they chose to carry
Can you imagine having a baby with him
or getting married?
If you can't then please tell me sister
why he gets the crown of a king
while walking around the house
with satanic energy?
Don't you know angels are
demons favorite treats?
Trading your halo of faith
for the pleasures of deceit
But they don't last forever,
as the high comes down
Rise does the need for a stronger dosage
like the addiction of a fiend
I know you know what I mean
Sister don't judge me
You could track those very lines
in mine and your history
Have we not both cut the strings
of this satanic puppetry?
Have we not both felt the sting

of realizing, you never healed
just numbed the reality?
Too hooked on the ability to
flourish through pain to be happy
Subconsciously victimizing
self to the maze, passively
While holding aggression toward
their ways of blasphemy
Which turn did you take
that finally made you see
there is beauty in the gravity
of being on your own two feet?
No longer letting the past
tangle you in the present
while still collecting all the jewels
you have found, in each lesson.

The Beautiful Me

In the pitch dark
I dived through every layer
down to the deepest part of your soul
just to see that treasure
Now I understand why I've stayed so long
For the endless possibilities
of what could be inside
I knew it was there
if I could get past the ego
you vicariously lived through
to reach for that key
I was suffocating
just to rehabilitate your sense of self
all the while losing mine
I wanted to peel away
those layers of deep denial
not so I could hurt you
but so I could heal you
so we could heal us
by synchronizing our deeper connections
being polluted at the surface like a massive oil spill
Delusional off the high of your own imbalance
This opposite complex was like, living in a fun house
So much mystery to the things I loved about you
like a sunken ship I was just dying to explore
to discover all the gem's no one ever did before
But was it worth giving up my lung capacity?
I could go but so long before coming up for air
Now and then you gave me a reason to go back there
Risking my health just to be the one
Staying a little longer, each time
until my body gave out
My spirit found me floating at the top
No longer concerned with this mission
but with survival

Instilling in me higher visions during its revival
Tell them I have no regrets
but have realized
the only treasure I need is
already in me
and I will no longer take for granted
what it means to breathe
What it means to just be,
the beautiful me.

REFLECTIONS

My Brown-Skinned Brother

Just as mine, his...
Brother-Sister ship was sinking
In you I found him, how astounding
My real brother, brown-skinned
We shared no womb, no blood, no marital relation
But you carried me through mud, past thugs, to elevation
Breast fed from bosoms of separate woman
whose paths never intertwined
Who would have thought our lives would bind
in ways too complex to verbalize
In the midst of tortured dreams,
you freed my spirit of morbid screams
Protecting me in every aspect as a brother should
Respecting me for all the assets, my brother never would
It was then I recognized, blood isn't thicker than
Remembering when my aggression
mentally seized up the trigger and

I reminisced, how he wished, almost did slit my throat
How he lost his grip when the cops had no pity to show
Chased with knives day in and day out of my life
I had made up my mind that his days now were mine
It was then I felt your warm embrace
as you said God's role I could not play
and one day he would look back
all those words, he'll wish he took back
Only could I push past,
in the arms of my brown-skinned brother
Without you I'd be just another number
Another woman under
imprisoned bars
with imprisoned scars
Victim to the cause
Swimming in his flaws
Because of you I've forgiven,
at his own loss
Because of you I am different,
your love's embossed in my heart.

I Remember

I remember sleeping with a weapon
by my bedside to protect myself
from my own flesh and blood
I remember being chased with knives
and told I was nothing but a worthless slut
That I, deserved to have my throat slit
And still years prior to that
I remember picking up the phone
overhearing him tell his friend
in response to his saying I was cute
"My sister? My sister's a slut!"
He didn't know my innocence
had been stolen two weeks before
He didn't know what those words meant
to a girl who'd just been raped
He didn't know that spreading rumors
to the whole city about me, was a big mistake
He didn't know how badly,
I needed him to be a real big brother
I remember when the cops came
I remember when my family blamed
me for his foul way
Well I could go on with remembering
but now I just pray he will be saved
I'm not sure how many years it's been
since we've truly spoken
His mere presence left around me such a bitter taste
that instead of healing, I'd gone numb to the pain
but when he was in the hospital
after surgery, I still went to visit
even though to me he was
just another abusive guy on the list
But the other day I realized
It's time to forgive
whether he has, or hasn't changed

Maybe he's sorry
and just doesn't know what to say
But either way, it's time to let it go
because the longer I don't,
I'm just stunting my own growth
So I wrote this poem not to remember all of his faults
but to remind myself that it would be my fault
if I went on living with hatred toward him in my heart.

Numbers in Mama's Shoes

Funny the places where truth be found
I wondered the faces of these hounds
The ones who broke my daddy's heart
The ones who stoned my family apart
Her face never revealed
the names and numbers in her heels
I knew too much too young
For her lust I never bit my tongue
Friends she claimed
'Friends' who left her soul in shame
Gone to the 'store' until three in the morn
When I called her bluff, I only got scorned
Scorned for the misery she accompanied
Punished me, for her own sins
It sunk in me, she was no longer
the mother in that skin
Now she became a stranger,
I didn't want to know
To this day she'd fill with anger,
if she saw these words I wrote
But I love her so
I swear I do
I just don't know to where she flew
or what ran through her mind
as she had another man
in our kitchen those nights
As I looked into my daddy's eyes
I wondered how many
numbers in her shoes
it'd take to kill him inside
I wondered if my baby sister understood
where mommy went when by her side I stood
I wondered how my brother would become a man
Now I just wonder who I am
What's my role in a family with so much deceit?

She sold her soul like candy every time she'd cheat
As I look for a man to be, I wonder how I will greet
How do I introduce him to a woman so cold?
As I seduce him, I wonder does he know
the complex pain my past withholds
Grasping onto him for what I never had at home
For a love the numbers in mama's shoes, never showed.

Grandma

If I could flip the hour glass,
take this hour back
Lord, you know I'd do just that
What I'd give to have her back
Never spent enough time
listening to her wise stories
Even as a Cancer survivor,
she always took on everyone else's worries
It all becomes so blurry, sometimes in life
Rush, rush
Hurry, hurry
Keep your eye on the prize
Next thing you know
on the other end of the line
They are telling you,
"She passed away last night."
Why didn't I visit her more
when I had a chance to be with her?
Kept saying each weekend
how I've missed her and should stop by
I don't know why
I've no alibi good enough to justify or describe
reasoning for not being at her side
All she wanted was a little time
to teach me things she liked
How to make those pretty necklaces,
with fancy beads she'd buy
Was it too much to put an hour or two aside?
Will our pitiful souls ever be forgiven?
Mistakes we all make and regret too late
Bargain our fate, placing bets with our days
Moments to be cherished in more productive ways
We all see the months perish but it doesn't change
Taking them for granted all the same
Grandma I'm ashamed and embarrassed for this fault

I could blame so many things for those chances lost
I could scream in vain and vouch my cause
But it wouldn't bring blood through your veins
and that's all I want
but your eyes are shut more firmly
then I've ever seen
Frankly Queen,
I'm not worthy of your resting in peace
Because so selfishly, I only think
of what it'd be to have you back
instead of being happy,
you're free from the pain at last.

If Mama Had Been There

If mama had been there, would she have told me
I was too beautiful to sacrifice myself to you?
Would she tell me wearing shoes that don't fit,
causes damage not bliss, and tendons
have a tendency to bend the way they're squished,
appearing as something different once suffocated
and one too many tongues bit, is the reason
woman stoop to being silenced
Wind up in a predicament of
verbal, physical, or emotional violence
If she hadn't chosen the numbers in her shoes
before being a mother
Would this have minimized the number of fools
I let use and abuse a heart of gold
while she was on the roam
Does she know her roaming minutes
ran out a long time ago?
After years of seeing my daddy die in the kitchen
over and over again while another man sat beside her
I've learned the beauty of mute
As a matter of fact it became my favorite button to press
so she couldn't press mine
Tell me why I feel nothing when she attempts
to express a love I never could find
Searching for the goddess I knew when I was nine
Daddy was searching for his bride
Tangled in the vines of her garden of bull s---
They say the most magnificent roses grow out of this
but that doesn't mean I don't remember the stench
while being the back bone for a battered husband
playing the role of both sexes to build from family destruction
Provide my baby sister with something she left us without
I kept pumping, trying to fuel the family
but somehow she always managed to get us on E
until there was no more energy

Being a kid but having to
fill a woman's shoes like I'm thirty
with no woman figure there to mentor me
Too busy protecting everyone while men hurt me
Now I must cleanse years of infestation
Mend my fears of marriage
and quit settling for guys I know I'd never
Subconsciously sacrificing my chances of being wedded
Keep thinking my head is, in a better place
But then why am I in a love triangle today
like still riding tricycles when you know
two wheels is the real way
This psychological, biological,
game of dominoes has to go
because it just isn't right
I know I must forgive her
because if I don't I'll never outlive her
and the more I try not to be like her,
the more I'd have been her
This is my heart without a sensor,
but sometimes I still think
if mama had been there,
I'd have been somewhere better.

Longing to be Loved

Longing to be loved
Not knowing how long love will be
How many reincarnated selves
until his arrival to my realm?
Impatiently patient, I am waiting
Lost like a glass slipper
Striving to nurture faith in the most-high,
while inside this corridor
or on this path per se
Sometimes I contemplate turning back another way
I think about whom I've left behind
and I wonder if I'm simply after him
in another time, another life, another physical shell
Will he return if I've gone too far?
Will I find out he was the perfect fit after all?
Will karma trace her way to me through his broken heart?
Who sent me here in the first place?
My endless array of questions form a hurricane
Chakras in overdrive, clash like tectonic plates
Hungry for balance, feed me!
Clarify my mental bowels
of the toxic need to see, future probabilities
Let me be content instead with possibility
Let me not be tempted by psychic abilities
Lusting for wisdom without the knowledge to get there
Free me of conditioning, revenge, and despair
I am tired of living how I used to
Even if finding me means I must lose you
Being truthful is a dirty job done by the cleanest souls
People throw away pruned fruit due to the flaws that show
But lies come shiny and smooth
when it's too good to be true
We buy them anyway,
convinced a bruise is a sign of decay
Society throws us away and calls us artists

then puts us on display to entertain, no longer garbage
In the spot light we're like lost and found pomegranates
Limits and boundaries extend far beyond the projects
We've got cotton fields for minds,
we are our masters and our slaves
Picking our own brains at an inhuman pace
Shackled by thoughts of time gone to waste
While longing to be loved,
we must reconstruct
what our self-destruct interrupted
To progress, expectations must be vanished
We are what we project on this planet
No wonder heartache and abuse
cling to us like magnets
I'm my own worse menace
See there be consequences for leaving thyself neglected
If I don't love and respect me, I'll never truly get it
Pain and suffering is mankind's sickest fetish
We push away what we need
because the poison holds appeal
Sometimes it's like we just want to be ill
But now I'm at a point where I just want to feel
Feel for me what he feels for me
If I'm not complete
How will I love somebody equally?
See I'm longing to be loved,
not knowing how long love will be
but I know it all begins when I start loving me.

Beautifully Insecure

A moment of personal revelation, please indulge
For I am a person of hesitation as is he with the bulge
All humanity, man and woman
condone a world of vanity whether good or bad looking
All I see are facades,
masked bruises underneath a Maybelline face
It's not a phase, it's the American ways
It's your fortieth birthday, better dye those grays!
Is there any limit to the price we'll pay?
It's apparent, we're all purely impure
Some days I want to care less, be beautifully insecure
Until the magazine aisle reminds me of my standards
Let's dream for a while that we were all blind, now answer
How is it we would judge each other then?
Like books with no covers to perceive reflection
Ceased would be our need to achieve perfection
or would we find another way to depict
Would plastic surgeons go out of business?
The questions arise,
one day I questioned why I'm so self-critical
You'd think being told your fly as hell
would make a person less miserable
and it does... just a little
Until you realize that no matter what you do
there's always an airbrushed diva that looks better than you
And most men couldn't care less
who's got real or fake breasts, facial reconstruction
No they just see what's in their face and now all of a sudden
delusional expectations are placed
While his queen is losing hope, she can't compete in that race
How can she be up to par with something that's fake?
Isn't that where female hate came into play anyway?
The "I wish I had...," list
I wish I had the strength to be sure
I wish I didn't have to pretend

not to be beautifully insecure
just like any other who walks this green earth
If we could relieve our thoughts of that green curse
Jealousy is the Devil
It's those whom love self that are on God's level
still we settle, for this nonsense
spoon fed to us like we're brain dead
Wounded self-esteem should be the picture painted
to represent this society of make believe
white picket fenced by lies that make us be incomplete
I'd rather be, beautifully insecure
I'd rather breed a world where it's okay to show hurt
Where when you tell your baby girl it's okay to be her
You're not another hypocrite among the many
Poisoned with the visual while holding glasses half-empty.

When I Forgot How to Smile

There was a time when I forgot how to smile
or what it meant to smile and truly feel it
When all I had was pain behind dimples
that couldn't explain even a little
of what I had been through
Ask me if I was okay, I'd have lied to you
Told you everything was fine
Hoped to God you couldn't see
the tears dripping from my pupil dilating eyes
as I tried to sell myself that same lie
while feeling naked like in a nightmare on stage
where the audience reminds you,
you forgot your clothes
Like every hole in my soul were exposed
for people to swim through
Finding the secrets of the internal mysteries
I couldn't expose such as my will being stole
On that road this gift of poetic lyricism
was the only thing that kept me living
when all I wanted to do was die
but didn't have the guts to slit my wrists
swallow pills, or jump into the sky
with shattered wings that couldn't fly
Much too human for that flight
And God told me it was my calling
to heal minds with the words I write
But it took repeated episodes of stalling
before I could finally
get in the studio or grab the Mic
Reading your diary to the world
or even to a small crowd
is not easy on your tender wounds
So I hid my talent for thirteen years
only publicly revealing it on websites
like, Rap Sheets and Hip Hop Poetry

or spitting for friends at a party
or to the few real cats who really
believed in me
Laced me with beats to record tracks
just to season me
and now I've surpassed that
fear that was eating me alive
Nearly defeating me
You see for a time the gift was a burden
while still serving the purpose
of freeing me from hurting
for moments of zone drifting
where I could let go
of all the hardship that had me imprisoned
Didn't really tell nobody
because I didn't think they would listen
but most of all I didn't want the pity
or to spread my pain in them
Felt like I was contagious
like I had some case of emotional Aids
but if you travel through the pages of
my life you'll surely trace
the deep roots beneath that pain
and understand why my smile now
shines bright like the sun after rain
Why I'm glowing in the face while radiating
this positive energy from my veins
circulating with life for the first time
since childhood days
before innocence was erased
and replaced with the rage
that took a while to tame
and brought more pain in more ways
Now it's a new day, but it feels like a new life
Like a second chance to make it right

with the experiences to ignite
the wisdom needed to survive this time
As I'm, facing every fear
Evaluating where I'll go from here
Reincorporating faith in my sphere
No longer scared to shift gears
and shine like the star
I always was through the tears
I can say that my smile ear-to-ear is sincere
Regardless of the parts of me
that must still heal
My heart is finally finding peace
in the way being happy feels
See it was easier to be broken when
that was all I knew for so long
but even when I was broken
my will was strong
Let nobody tell me I would be
damaged goods forever on
I knew one day this day would come
if I kept pushing on
So here I am
Understand, it didn't happen over night
Don't miscalculate my present joy
for having an easy life
Just let me instill in you the messages
it took for me to be the light.

Real Men Have Feelings Too

Real men have feelings too
They break down, kneeling down
crying to God when times are rough too

All men aren't bad
despite the bad things I've been through
There are good men out there
and I know a few...
But they serve different purposes
in my life and that's cool

Big brothers, guardian angels, a father-figure too
To all of these men, I say, "God thank you!"
Even though I haven't met my husband,
I'm still grateful, to know these men sent by you

Every time I catch myself thinking
that there is no good man for Tabu
I remind myself,
"Real men have feelings too!"
Wait, let me say it one more time
Real men have feelings too
They feel the same ways we do
Every man isn't here to hurt, use, and abuse you

Even though if we round out the ratio
of good men, and bad men
The percentages
of the good men I've dated
verses the relationships
horrible enough to lead me to salvation
when I was at my breaking...
my breaking point

Sliding down that cliff
with nobody to tell me
I was too beautiful for this

And let me tell you,
it's sometimes still so hard
to look back at all my faults
The times I stayed, a little too long
The times I knew better,
but was just so gone
Cause' what was in my mind
wasn't what was in my heart
What I saw with my eyes
wasn't what I felt
when all I felt was their arms
It was all I knew of love
even when it was the snake charm
to make me fall
and I fell

Even when my girls said
I was too pretty and smart
There were times,
I allowed men to isolate me
from my whole circle
Oh, there were times I dissed family
There were times when canceling plans
for some man was expected from me
Forgive me

But there were things
nobody could see
Such as those times
when all I could do was cry

and didn't want them
to see me like this
cause' I,
couldn't even look myself
straight in the eyes
and say I was living right

See, I didn't have the guidance in my life
I didn't grow up with somebody
telling me all the things I could be if I just tried
I didn't know the Godly role of being a wife
But I tried my best to be lady-like
Had morals, but I also had
something going on deep inside...
like a disease spiritually killing me,
paining me all the time
Allowing me to be re-victimized
Like I was magnetic to these type of guys

I let the rapist win for so many years
I asked myself "Why???"
Told myself every year,
it would be different this time
I would fight
I would no longer be a victim
I'd survive
But then I'd be
caught up in another situation
Adding more bondage
to these demonic ties

And although I always loved me some good guys
It seemed like I never had one for myself
Because I thought I was ruined inside
and didn't love myself enough to cry for help

Times I wanted to die, all by myself
Times I gave up on life, secrets I didn't tell
Times I wanted to hide, like a book on the shelf
Swore I'd never open, ever again
And then somehow I'd open, for these no good men

But I'm not the woman I was then
I'm not the young chick
who used to be out partying
until I learned the hard way
where that path led
I'm not the girl who was manipulated
by some older man in a relationship...
I will not be that woman again
Even though they are still chasing
my purity within

There will always be those brothers
who mistreat a lady, like how they mistreat their mother
Like how they mistreat another when you're gone
Looking for the next lamb, to butcher, brand, and toss

But I took the time to clear my thoughts...
In June 2010 I declared,
this would be the last year
that some abuser would break my heart
It was over
The curse was through

And even though I've been hurt,
I know real men have feelings too
I know not all men, are just after Tabu
with wickedness in them
like the men I was used to

I have seen my dad get played too
I've known good men,
and God I thank you

Though there were times when
I even wanted to hate you
Blame you, for letting bad men like this exist
Times I was angry, couldn't face the truth
that I needed to accept responsibility
and start making better choices

But first I needed
some deep rooted deconditioning
to begin to heal through things
and breathe again
before I would ever see
that men aren't all like this
I used to fear that every man
might be a rapist
and in a way that fear
did more damage than protection
when I wound up with
the wrong men over and over again
who picked up on my weakness
like a wounded deer,
just what they needed

But today is a new day
The day the Lord has made
August, 2010 I gave my life away
to Jesus Christ
and I have changed
I'll never be the same
Not to say there hasn't been heartache

But I'm free from every cage
No longer trapped inside that page
My diary can go on
Transition into new chapters

Yes this is my,
happily ever after
and it may not be perfect
but that doesn't matter
I'm waiting for a good man,
a man of God too
A real man who has feelings
and expresses them too
A man who communicates
A man who tells the truth
A man who can make
my dreams of real love come true

Don't ever underestimate
what God can do for you
Don't ever man-hate
because of what some
other brothers put you through

Ladies, guard your temples
and let those men go
Wait for a man
who will live by
the Biblical principles

Wait for a real man who
will let his feelings show
Yes, he will...
and this I know.

They See

They see your smile, they see your elegance
but they don't see all the emptiness
Go home at night when the show is all done
Take off the fishnet tights, pearls, and makeup
Practically crawled up those stairs to your room
The audience is no longer there, it's just God and you
Never too weak to pray, but you feel too weak to praise
You feel so worthless, so alone at the end of the day
You have all the love and then you have nothing at all
You have one million friends, and then you have just one
Do you even have one? I don't know anymore
Would they be there when you need some cash
because your car needs to be repaired?
The artistry don't seem to pay, it just don't pay
at least not in the state you live in anyway
Back on nine-to-five thoughts of hunting for a job
Unemployment checks are running up
Darn... this isn't what I want
Everything just seems to keep going wrong
Almost getting jumped last week, and now the car
Plus a stalker making fake pages of you
Trying to ruin your career, before it barely starts
Some people, they treat you like a super star
but they don't really know what's in your heart
Shining star, feel like you're only shining on stage
then you fall... fall into the velvet skies
that become the blankets where you hide
Hold your pillow late at night and cry,
asking God, "Why?"
No matter how hard you try,
trouble seems to follow you
The enemy keeps taunting you
What's your game plan? I don't have one
Lord, I didn't know
all these things would go wrong

By now I should know, been through it all
Still more to come,
Lord please give me your protection
Stop the spread of this infection, eating away at my mind
I can't slip back into depression, those days I've left behind
I'm running out of time, the clock keeps ticking faster
louder, the hands poking harder at my thoughts
I was lost then I was found and now I'm... lost
Does it make any sense?
All of this confusion,
I don't even know where to begin
Every time I'm winning, I'm losing
and I'm so tired of playing a game
that wasn't even my choosing
I'm too real for this earth's surface
It's so hard to be present
I catch myself frequenting the spiritual realm
I like it better than that beautiful hell
What has mankind done to your creation?
Every time I turn on the news, it's another rapist
Another woman had her fetus ripped out
Another murder in the streets
Another mother holding her head,
covered in the blood of her son
Another club shot up, what the hell is going on?
Husbands killing their whole families,
Leaving apologetic letters on the desktop
You're sorry you just shot your children?
Sorry you just, stabbed your wife to death?
Get all of this ugliness out of my head
I don't want to see it anymore
The Devil's work is done as the rain pours
when Jesus cries and the tears start
rolling out my own eyes
So many people committing suicide and we shame them

like we don't understand why, but I understand why
I've been there before
Curled up in a ball on the floor
Barely sixteen felt like a stolen dream
Knife to wrist and what saved me? Poetry.
Everybody jokes about rape, but it was no joke to me
The women in South Africa surely aren't laughing
The man in New Haven
who said his daughter was gang raped
doesn't think it's a joke
I could name so many lives Satan keeps jacking
It isn't just rape, that's just one example of demonic passion
Some people want to know
why I talk about it in some of my poetry
because I got tired of being quiet
just for other people's ignorant, blissful needs
We've got needs too, don't you see? We need to heal!
People are hurting worse than the masks that conceal
We're all doing good when you ask us, but on some real
We all have a messed up story to tell
We weren't born on silver platters
like white America sells
We're all a bunch of Broadway actors
playing our parts very well
They don't see you in the morning time
with your eyes swell
Teardrop syndrome, eyes looking rusty
like they just got out of prison
Hair looking so crazy
and your migraine got the left eye twitching
Thinking to yourself...
“I better get to fixing!"
Run to the bathroom, hang your silk robe on the hook
Turn on the shower, hot water... steam it up real good
You wish you were at the spa but this will have to work

Yes this will, this will have to do
until this artistry starts paying you
Standing there, looking at your naked reflection
Wondering if there is a man who could love you
when you are stripped of the glamour they keep sweating
Would he be there to relieve the stressing?
Would he be showering you with affection?
More than sexing... slowly, softly, like heaven
and would he keep pressing
things you shared about your past
or would he be helping you heal from all of that?
Would he take out the trash or bring more?
Would he fall in love too fast and then
leave when he's bored?
Where is my mind going? Still got the shower running
Hurry, jump in before the hot water runs out
I don't do cold showers, I'm getting in now
Wash away the night, it's a new day
Soap my body repeatedly, I feel so dirty
So filthy from letting the enemy hurt me
I need to trust God a little more
so that Satan can't burn me
I feel the burns like third degree, inside of me
All of this scrubbing isn't doing nothing
but at least I'll be clean
They'll say I smell so good and I'll smile thankfully
but they won't know what I just dealt with
that nearly disfigured me internally
Even got a foot scrub for my feet
from them stilettos I've been wearing all week
We're always searching for the better remedy
to hide the imperfections that may possibly
reveal our humanity
Nobody will even know I had a rough day yesterday
They'll just see the pretty, in their face

They probably wouldn't care anyway
I don't need nobody to pity me
but it'd be nice to have some real friends
to be there for me when the show ends
and it's all gone
Where is the man to give me a massage?
They say I can have any man I want
Maybe that's true
but I need a man who will say "I do"
This abstinence thing is not easy for a woman who
has a volcanic sexuality, ready to erupt like hot lava
on the first man who, crowns me queen
Rock me sound to sleep, I'm just a baby
when all of this womanhood
gets worn down to vulnerability
Too strong for my own good
but if they could see
there is so much more beyond the look, to me
Somebody, somebody's got to see me
I can be a lot of things on my own
but I need a king
and some true friends
who aren't just after me romantically
and a crew who has my back
when the haters attempt to damage me
When all of this vanity
shimmery eye candy
lip gloss, eye cream,
and face powder comes off,
it's just me and God.

Feelings and Thoughts

I compressed my already expressed
but still freshly pressed,
feelings and thoughts in an airtight box
Suffocated.
I've forgotten how to climb out of the top
Now I'm suffering with a heart made of locks
I scream only to find oxygen wasted
Nobody can hear me. I can't take it.
I've been abandoned
even though
my physical body's still standing
around crowds of folks
My spirit and soul are in this place
and nobody knows
They can hear my voice
but they can't hear,
me banging against my insides
It doesn't matter how clear I try to make it
I'm still Miss Misunderstood of the year
Spiking the party punch with my emotions
as a tear rolls down my eye
and nobody noticed
It's like I'm invisible all over again
It's like every time I let somebody close
I'm taken for granted
I remember an abuser of my past
once rationalized the reasons why
people try to hurt me all my life
before I knew he'd be another
abuser, in due time
Naive. Age sixteen as this man told me
"It's because you're beautiful,
that's why they do it,"
and you know
sometimes, I like that excuse

but the truth is
maybe it's because they are ugly
and I always tried
to see the beauty in everybody
Some folks say they love me
and some of them do
But I believe there are some things
love just doesn't do
I am tired of being on mute
for speaking the truth
Looking for the right clue
to lead them to where they can find
the rest of me in an ice cube
So blue, so cold
How long was I frozen?
They don't know
But it feels like centuries
in my feelings and thoughts
Maybe it's only been hours
Maybe days
But ask my pain in this moment
Feels like the hourglass is broken
and the contents of salt and glass pieces
made a promise that this would stab the deepest
as the sting claims to disinfect
but it feels like I'm being poisoned
Just wondering when someone
will find my skeleton
when it's like I don't exist
and I've never liked boxes
so how did I manage to lock myself in?
This doesn't make sense
Lord I repent for my frantic reactions
when every breath feels like this might be it
and that tiny crack letting light in feels torturous

I can see them but they can't see me
Not from this view point, at least
As I fall asleep, falling weak
Praying for a prince to come kiss me
Maybe I'm sleeping beauty
and nobody told me
Maybe you'll be the one to hold me
Bring me to myself
Maybe you enjoy dusty book shelves
with ancient secrets untold
about the girl whose heart and soul
disconnected from her flesh
and didn't know where to go
Ran away to this hiding space
and now I can't come out
until God says it's time for me to be found
Optimistically I think,
"Maybe He doesn't want anybody
to kick me while I'm down,"
and while it seemed like this was all my fault
maybe God put me in here so we could talk
Trying to see the glass half-full
even when the last drop is all I can see
I know I must leave this to God and let myself go
so if all you find are fragments of the old me and this poem
Please know that these words are not the last words I wrote
and take a real good look around
for a better woman than the one I was
when I felt all alone and for a second lost hope
that He would carry me home
I guess He just taught me a lesson of survival
to call on him just a little more
Cause' what if I was one prayer too short
Just talk to him when I'm feeling torn
by a world so cruel

Just let Him pick out the thorns
and be still for a few
Don't rely on no man for what God can do
Just wait on Him
He always comes through
Sometimes He's got to break you
out of your comfort zone
So He can make you stronger
Even when you get emotional, don't lose focus
Keep your eyes on him
In this life, it's sink or swim
so I chose to rise with Him
when the walls were closing in
He heard my heart still belonged to Him
even if my feelings and thoughts had me trippin'
when He boxed me in just to bring me out
and remind me of all the times He gave me a way out.

In Her Giver

There's a place in me I just can't describe...
As long as I've been writing poetry
digging into my mind
Letting the ink of my diary,
leak all over pages, of my life
I've seemingly let the whole world look into my eyes
I've put my heart on the podium, swallowed my pride
I've painted audiences, with my soul... so, so many times...
But I can't tell you why
There is this part of me that hides
I think it's time to release her, let her full light shine
I'm scared if I don't keep her, that they will try
to take what is mine
Taint the purity I held onto
through everything I've survived
They wouldn't understand
It wouldn't make any sense
How could a grown woman,
still behold, a little innocence
Still dreams how she used to dream
Before people tried to, blow the fuse in me
Thought they took all of my electricity
They thought the lights went out
But they forgot, night owls like the dark
So what you can't see now
I just buried and stashed back inside of my heart
and the thing that gets me the most
is that the community needs
these things in me to show
They need more than my poems
They need me to reach out to them
so we can grow
And I know all of my gifts need to be honed
because Lord I can't do this alone

I'm trying Lord, you know I am
Open up that door, put my trust in your hands
Truly expose all I am
Not just all of my talents
but all of the woman I've become
You know I want to show them, who I once was
I wish there was a simple way
to show them what it took for me to be here today
It may not seem like much just yet
But I'm making progress
Soon I will be successfully accomplished
And the truth is that it won't mean nothing
if I didn't make a difference in someone's life
Lord, I said none of this won't mean nothing...
if I didn't change, save somebody
through the things I write
I need to know I'm being received
when I'm rocking these Mic's
Anybody can applaud me, when the lines sound tight
But if at the end of the night
if all I have to show for is books sold and money made
then I haven't done my job even if I'm being paid
See I want more than just a little fame
I don't want to be just another poetess face
Even though people approach me every day
Reassuring me that my words are doing God's work
and have helped them through, the hurt
that they run to my poems, during the worst
Lord, you know it feels good
But somehow I feel I'm not giving my all
that if I can heal people by showing half my cards
then imagine what I can do when I deliver
the entirety of the gifts you've given me
Not just words written, but let them sink deeper into me

Set me free, so I won't worry about the stage
or think about, the opinions being made
Just let myself go so that I'm living those poems
the way that I lived them, when I wrote
Even if I have to pretend, I'm in that room alone
Just me and God, like I'm invisible
And though there are split seconds
where I've gotten to that level
with my poetic expression
There are far too many moments
when I hold onto this
piece of gravity beneath my feet
I've always performed passionately
but there's something more in me
Something to be seen beyond the ordinary
standards of great poetry
Something that can increase the feedback
from folks whose souls feel me
It's time to break through the surface
and forget about being perfect
My heart is burning away all the walls
You'll be amazed that
even in my transparency
on the pages where it comes easily
I still kept up my guards on these stages, see
For too long I gave them just enough
Just enough to love me in hope that
the substance in each piece was enough
to mean something more than just poetry
You know this is where my heart will always be
and these words were never just words to me
So it's time to be more intimately engaged
with God while in that
"Lights, Cameras, Action," mind frame
It's time to be brave

Let Him move me
how He wants to, without shame
Don't be afraid of who I intimidate
Just let it reign
Take over each and every vein
Fully breathe each word I say
until I create a sea of waves
flowing to the rhythm
of the beat from which I'm made.

The Ultimate Decision

I've decided...
I want to be more than a performer
I want to be a provider
More than another poet
who can rip sick metaphors
No see I want to take this higher
As a matter of fact,
this poem doesn't even need to rhyme
and I don't always have to feature
with pieces I've memorized
although it is my preference
More important than the applause
is reaching somebody's heart
Even if it's just the woman in the back row
clinging to your words like life support
when she's suicidal and nobody knows
just how close she has been to that ledge
Just how many fantasies
she's had about being dead
to the extent where her entire life
has revolved around them
until the moment she heard something you said
Maybe just one line, the one you usually forget
Improvising, cause' you know the golden rule
Nobody knows your poem but you
But this time you got it right
Maybe lost another
Got hard on yourself for it after
but didn't know
you just saved somebody's mother or
sister, or significant other
or the lady on the right who just lost her brother
Sometimes we don't realize
how many stories are in that room
while we're busy telling our own

I'll be rocking Mic's for life but
these poems are more than poems
More than finger snaps when you spit fire
More than approval
from fellow poets who feel inspired
No see...
These poems are life preservers
Relationship healers
Love and light workers
Deliverance inducers
Concubine-to-Queen producers
Make a sister change her life
and stop acting stupid
Make a brother think before he slips up
Stop someone, somewhere from giving up
Even if it's just one
So who cares if half the poetry scene hates me
I'm human they don't have to praise me
I have to trust that God has me on this mission
Not for nothing even if
it doesn't lead to fame and fortune
I will know that I kept the essence in my poetry
Not to mention I've been warned, prophetically
not to compromise when they want to commercialize me
I take that seriously as I make the ultimate decision
to be more than the performer but to be the provider
Spoken word artist slash preacher
The student and the teacher
Every brother and sister's keeper
Truth speaker
More than just a crowd pleaser
I've decided to believe in the reason I am here
and not to be deceived by the show
when that is just the medium being used
to reach the people's ears

Honestly, I'm still facing fears
Still get butterflies on stage
Still get nervous I'm going to
lose my place or forget what to say
Thanking God when it all goes smooth
but most of all I'm thanking God
if my words reach you
because mastering performing
means nothing
if that piece means nothing to you
But even if it doesn't,
at least I can save myself.

Ready

My toes are tingling
I've never felt this feeling before
Butterflies roaming my body
beyond my stomach, all through my core
My mind is racing
I try to stop it
but it breaks through every net
and keeps going on this quest
I'm naked of ego, and even more blessed
I'm humbled and don't care about being the best
Well, at least not better than you
It isn't about getting ahead of you
My competition is myself, to rise
to be a better me
then I could be yesterday
If I can rise above the old me
then surely the enemies
working against me are all a phase
Soon I won't be concerned
with anything but putting God first
Soon I'll live each and every word
Man's hands only break things, mistake things
The only perfection of my humanity
is the God in me
It is no use making promises I can't keep
so I ask God to guide me as I
feel the anticipation happening all over again
times a million, like when I first entered the scene
Will they love me?
Will they hate me?
Will they believe?
Will they be part of my movement
to bridge the gap and set love free?
Can I, can we, come together as a team
Building pyramids

around new found wisdom
and manifested dreams
One brick at a time, to the top
I can't press rewind, and I can't press stop
I keep going, I keep flowing, to the next track
leading me to the next path to reach a destination
that will lead me through another journey
to a bigger equation
Living each day like pages of a book
After the first chapter, I was hooked
through the bad and the good
If it were too good to be true,
I would know it was false
but in this case
when the work is done,
it has just begun
I'm going crazy half the time
But I know I can keep my sanity
if I can keep my eyes on the prize
If I can possess a piece of sunshine inside
to pull me through the rain outside
Lord knows there is plenty of it
pouring down on the diary of my heart
and every time I see the ink smudge
I'm so afraid of a new start
Until I see, it's all working out after all
It's so hard,
and I'm so soft,
and so scarred
but so pure,
and so found
but so lost
I never thought
this day would come
I thought it was too late

Now it feels just right
as the fruits bear their truth
that everything will be okay
Every missing piece to my puzzle
will find its way
until I may reap the beauty
of the whole picture
Once it's made,
I wonder
if these butterflies
in my toes
will fly ever fly away
and if I'll miss them
until they come back again
I wonder if they are angels
keeping me floating on clouds
across skies, to this place
away from
the rock.

She's Crafty

She's crafty
like a crescent moon
lighting the whole city
in the midst of glittery stars
dripping with wishes
like hot glue on fabrics
that never quite stick
how you want them to
but for her, it's no issue

She's crafty
like henna paint designs
inking creations of divine
on skin created by divine

Crafty like butterflies
in bellies of little girls
with big dreams
growing up to be
women with broken
wings, from painful realities
But see, she knows just the thing
to fix these, make them fly again

She's crafty
like collective poems
written by segregated hands
Like unity for split moments
Like stilettos broken in
by escapades of freedom
marked by each scuff
but she has just the trick
when no one else does
to make the old new
as wardrobe malfunctions

become fashion do's
before don't can even
slip from dull lips,
that never quite get
what it means to live

Crafty is who she is
It's her culture
like Hip-Hop to B-Girls
Like beat box on street blocks
laced by sixteen bars
of a freestyler
as corners become
stages for rising superstars
right from the concrete
like the rose that grew,
she is...
illuminating
her craft within
Lighting the whole city
with her passion
Pursuing the destiny
for which she was crafted.

Summer Maiden

She wanted the sun to kiss her lips
As the wind, toy with her sundress
reminding her of innocence
of childhood...
of running through the sprinkler
with friends
just to see the rainbow
Oh what it meant.

She remembered those days
when everything had substance
Retained true meaning,
yet meant nothing

It was all so easy, untainted
All the things she dreamed to be
She could do it if you could name it

There were no obstacles
standing in her way
Imagining her favorite popsicle
brought a smile upon her face
Good old simplicity, easing away pain

She could tell you the things
that agonized her today
But would it even matter?

She'd rather
submit herself to
quenching the thirst
of the universe
like a lemonade stand
Squeeze something out
that would be worth more

then souls that had
been bargained
been bought and
been sold
Been bruised and
been shown
pathways of hopelessness

If only she could show them
the things she will know tomorrow
Oh, just let her drift again
Surely, she'll come up
with a cure for all the sorrow
Win back the world, we borrowed...

But then she could live in the moment
when it was all hers on repeat
Like a song that never gets old
Play it until you can sing it
in your sleep
Hymning her way back to
inner peace

The grass was green between her feet
Tickled softly, in the rhythm
of nature's melody
Chin to the sky, yellow
from buttercup games

She held no shame
Fell in love
with the sun
as it painted her face
and dyed her hair
shades of red and honey browns

Beauty back then
was more profound
The marks of life
on your skin
The effortless
spark in your eyes
shined from within

The bottle-less
divinity
that no
artificial fixation
could replace

How fast things can change
The secrets of happiness
forgotten
in the land of
robotic motions
Turning folks rotten
bitter, sour lipped
She promised herself,
she wouldn't be like this

Don't trip...
She'd been broken
Been through it
She knew the feeling
of forced memories
between her hips

Self-esteem
damaged
and the transition
to self-sabotaging
in destructive
relationships

Knew a life loveless
in a time before
when the hymning birds
caged inside, couldn't soar
That feeling
when you can't
take no more

But she held onto
what she was born for
and gave birth to
words that
could end the wars
executing our minds

The real battles fought
without guns
or men dying
on the frontlines
The kind where,
the only one dying is you

So she became a queen
of solitude
Rebelled humbly
Remained serene
Spoke truth
Drank tea, radiated youth

She wouldn't be
dried out by
society's inadequacies
She refused...

as she
kicked off
her shoes
and danced
upon the dirt
Letting pureness
protrude
the way it once did

when the
summer sun
first kissed
her lips.

Remember Me

Wipe the lip gloss off
Peel away the eye candy
Take off the earrings
Take off the rings
except the one
symbolizing celibacy
Put the crown of royalty
away for safe keeps
deep inside of me
in a place where
one million angel
heart's beat spiritually
Take off the stockings
and sparkly stilettos
Run the bubble bath
with rose petals
and white candles
Pick out something comfy
silky, and sweet
Write a love letter
on the mirror that says
"Thank you Jesus
for reminding me to love me!"
Pretend to forget
to erase it from the glass
then see it one morning
when you are feeling so bad
and smile again,
maybe even laugh
as you reminisce on
the memory looking back
to those wholesome moments
in between all the pain
The microphone couldn't
expose all the blood in my veins

that poured from the heavens,
sealing my heart when it breaks
See I'm just me at the end of each day
Love me for what you see
or love me for more
then just my face
More than my body
More than poetic words that trace
the outlines of my testimony
like Jesus' fingers on my lips
when the tears linger and then slip
from my eyelashes
and he catches every single one
Remember me,
more than a poetess
but a live
breathing
woman.

God Chosen Poetess

Friendships are ending, the earth is breaking
Somewhere right now there is a poetess
who can't finish her sentence on stage
in front of an entire audience waiting
Just seconds ago they were snapping
shouting, with exclamations
But times are changing
Humanity has its way of making an in
at that moment when you think
you have it all together
but then comes the pressure
Oh Lord...
They can't see you when you hit that floor
They don't care why your eyes look
more tired than before
Up fighting, crying, battling these wars
And when you miss a line
When you, begin to cry right there on the Mic
When you feel every word inside
They think it's all just an act, right on time
But they had no clue
You were still living that moment
This piece was the truth
Every page of your diary exposed
for people to criticize upon, lie on
Search your weaknesses
and try to stop you so you can't shine on
Love, you are the sun rising
You are the beauty
and this world is the beast
You are the ruby my virtuous queens
These men can't jack up our careers
Have us shedding tears
Distracted from all the years
we've put in just to get right here

If he loved you he'd want to help you steer
But you see the agenda all along
was to make you surrender
Fall off that mountain,
took you a lifetime to climb
Don't underestimate the intentions
in people's minds
Be careful, she's not your friend
from behind
But she will try to get your man
to take her from behind
Excuse me if I've crossed the line
Do I sound unladylike?
See I've, been rocking Mic's
for quite a while
People have seen me cry
and they've seen me smile
but they didn't know
I'm really going through trials
I've really been in situations
I'm an open book in a place of Satan
because he's everywhere that God is
Trying to rob this, he wants it
can't have it, I grab it, it's mine
It's time to start being human
Reach that point of desperation
See there was always this noise
when all I had was my pen
telling me to keep writing
Even when I felt like resigning
See each poem is from my heart, so play fair
Don't stomp on me when I'm bare
I'm thankful for what I have
even if it's only my pen and pad
At the end of the day, God gave me even that

I never planned to be a poet, that's a fact
Some folks are just following a fad
See this is something I can't just give back
This was a calling since age ten,
I had to live that
When the words started flowing,
I had to script that
The force was too powerful to contain
but I didn't know that everything
from my subjects to my name
was all, already made
All I'm really doing is cruising in my lane
And if you've never noticed
I am more than, but never less than
a God-chosen poetess.

DRAMA

Drama Free Means...

Bumping Mary J's joint in the whip one last time
as a means to counsel you through this one last time
you let anybody like that ever interrupt your life
You know misery loves company
Feeds off that down wrong energy
So when they get you in that place,
the street goes two ways
and then it's you to blame for staying
Played the game for a while
I'm sure the Devil found it knee-slapping funny
Drama has never been God's style
and it's looking quite ugly
No matter how you switch it up
It will never fit like love
Think I need a new wardrobe,
a change of clothes for my soul
Put my heart on stilettos,

get my mind done right
Get up out of dollar store mode,
cop some 'Gucci' sight
This isn't about the materialistic
It's about spiritual enrichment
Envisioning that place where you want to be
Remembering everyday
there's nothing stopping me
Nurture those seeds and faith will grow
Soon you'll find yourself in control
Naturally keeping weeds out of your harvest
No need for bitter pesticides,
just pull and toss it
Wherever your heart is,
know when to count your losses
Make way for the new light
Suddenly you'll hold the winning hand
Every time a lesson is learned in life,
you become the champion
And yes you "better know your friends,"
when people will use you like a good excuse
with no remorse for the things they do to you
Just in one heart valve and out the other
But there's a call I've got to take now
It's Drama Free on the line, brother.

Leave Me Alone, I'm Healing

The punishment for disturbing God's work
while healing the wounds of His child
are likely to be as severe as the punishment
to those who caused the bleeding
Have you forgotten what has been said
of the double edged sword? I question
While you are crow calling
wishing death upon your own brothers and sisters
Blood is blood when we all can trace back
to the same ancestor
not to mention, we're all human
or did you think you were immortal for
split seconds of ignorance
while you subtracted minutes from His mission
His vision for His child's future ahead
as you played advocate for Satan
Placing distractions in the way of success
Haven't you seen enough proof yet
of what happens when mankind tests
the most highs quests
rather than submitting to obedience
or are you even His children?
Which two God's are you serving?
Because last time I checked, there was only one
Might as well call yourselves Pagans
with the witchcraft games you've been playing
Might as well get used to your new home in hell
if this is the path you choose, to be rebels
When I tell you to leave me alone, I'm healing
You might want to consider what will occur if you don't
before you try to reel me in, crucify me for your own sins
When you saw Satan, that was your reflection
But since the Devil is a liar, I suppose the God in me
has your eyes in trickery, seeing things oppositely
But that ugliness was you, not me just for the record

Before you begin to fluff your feathers
Get all arrogant like you're someone better, remember
God can see right through you, which means I can too
Revealing things to me like whose who
Suddenly kings become peasants and queens become
demon infested practicing voodoo, claiming Christianity
Let me school you, there will be penalties
Don't let all the times you get away with it fool you
Don't think that repentance means acceptance
if the forgiveness from your lips
and heart add up difference
Something is missing, called sincerity
You'd do it all again, fearlessly
God fearing isn't even in your vocabulary
but yet God can take the gravity
from beneath your feet
have you buried six feet deep
before you get a chance to say, "I'm Sorry."
We're lucky God forgives, but this doesn't mean
we should take for granted the chances
I'm healing and you can't stand it
The thoughts of my happiness make you sick
You don't know what I've been through in my life
to even need this much deliverance
You're too busy pointing fingers
Judging and buying rumors
just to flip them on street corners
when the gossip is the hottest drug in
I'm wondering...
At which point does reality begin to plug in?
Before or after you must pay for your sins?
I'm wondering if you even know that love is
much bigger than hatred
which is why I'm unbreakable
Because God's love keeps me whole

No matter how many times you think
I'm going to stay and entertain the show
I'll get down on my knees to pray
and praise that much more
Unstoppable, powerful, spirit filled soul
So thankful, so humbled, I've won this war
Good against evil
No matter how many sequels
The Devil will lose
So now we know the side you choose
But I pray for my worst enemies
even when they've hurt me
I don't deserve to be pitied
I give the demons no glory of hate
Asking God to please take these thoughts away
Things my flesh would have liked to see done to yours
Asking Him to increase my capacity,
maximizing His presence more
Even in your declaration of war,
I've found it in me to say...
forgive them Father for their dishonor
Lord knows I wanna, throw some grenades
But these stages of deliverance
have me in a fragile place
where I must stay away from the frontlines
where Satan has his puppets on strings
moving how he likes
I must leave that stage for them to decide
if this is the life they're destined
or if they will cut the strings in due time
While everything inside of me begins to rise
like a peaceful volcano getting ready to erupt
I dare them to try to come between God's healing touch
as he brings the lava up, allowing me to purge all the hurt
Scorn, anger, rage, depression, and pain

I suggest you let God do His work and walk away
I can't control what he'd let happen
if you participate in foul play
So when you see me healing,
don't mistake me for fair game
Preying on what you perceive as vulnerability
will be your biggest weakness
with no more mercy to plea.

My Window Seat Thoughts

Well everybody doesn't have to understand me
but surely they can leave me alone
Never been out to hurt nobody
so tell me what on earth is going on?
Crucify me like my name was Jesus
Is it just because I'm different?
Has the scene become so tightly knit
that it's become robotic, cause' it's like
everybody acts like they are so conscious
then they do the same things they say aren't
Like when Eryka Badu came out with "Window Seat",
you really think you knew what she meant
but then you are doing the exact thing
Quick to assassinate what you don't understand
Take a look at the role you are playing
over and over again, what sense is it making?
Ignorance is the risk you are taking
This war isn't being fought with legitimate reason
Just a bunch of manipulated,
manipulating people speaking
trying to throw in their two cents
Nobody is getting rich off of this
Steady digging for a weakness just to take a hit
One day you'll be begging for forgiveness
One day you're going get to thinking
maybe you shouldn't have taken part in this
groupthink way of thinking
Maybe she's actually a good woman
just trying to make it, like anybody else
Just trying to focus on artistry and stay in good health
Go to church every Sunday, get prayed up
If I'm not performing, I'm in the crib writing new stuff
So what, what you mad at me?
Got to make up rumors
to change up the image they had of me?

Does my passion just eat you up inside?
My head never got big,
I'm more humble than I've ever been in my life
Just doing my own thing
Why do you have a problem with me?
Nobody had drama to bring when I wasn't shining
Funny how things change
All the games people play
Grapevine always coming with some bad grapes
that never quite make the wine
but they kind of get mixed up in the bucket sometimes
until somebody realizes, this one just isn’t looking right
If I could give them all a piece of mind, I'd say
I feel like I'm watching a child play follow the leader
like you all are just a little behind your years
Don't you think? A little bit low, don't you sink?
Don't you stoop when you do the things you do?
Now you've got a new reason to be mad at me
I'm telling the truth and I don’t have to lie
I'm more worried about satisfying the most high
then fitting in the little boxes
where you try to trap my pride
Don't you think it's time to get a life
Stop worrying about mine
Suppose you were to die today
What kind of legacy are you leaving for anyone to say
you really contributed to some kind of positive change
Told you all before, I'm not worth your stereotypes
I don't walk around
criticizing the canvas's on which you paint
Maybe you should stop deflecting
the self-changes you need to make
and start looking in the mirror of your own souls
because clearly I can't be held responsible
for the foul play in which you partake

Yeah, so what you made me feel a little heartache
Made me listen to "Window Seat" in a whole new way
Made me say...
now I get what she was saying
more than I did yesterday
As much as you may wish to put my dreams at stake
You can't control the choice God made
when he made me, when he gave me,
the destiny I'm pursuing
So you can hate me, try to break me
but nothing will stop me from doing
what I was put here for
Can't stop the Lord from blessing me with rewards
Your destruction can only go but so far before
it comes back around and you have to pay for
all the times you tried to destroy my creation
So I hope you enjoy this while you can
Because your day is waiting
As for me, I may run away from CT
Get me a "Window Seat" until somebody
saying that they miss me
I'll come back a little more relieved
ready for the next mission to complete
So before you all begin to think
that this is all the end of me
This, is just the beginning
I've just begun living
If you think I'm shining now
You'd better get some good shades
or start figuring out how to find your own way
We all have our own lanes
No need for jealousy or whatever this may be
Keep your chaos away from me
If you aren't spreading love,
I just don't need you around me

And if the bootleg cover serves you better
then the authentic version of me
then go ahead and continue to underestimate
the person inside that you don't see
I guess whatever sells in the street is what it'll be
I guess several attempts of
messing up my reputation
got them feeling mighty wealthy
on the ego tip
but I can see your spirits
look poorer than they ever did
while I continue to evolve,
walking right through the bullets
without any shame in being,
artistically naked.

How Dare They

How dare they
break your heart
and then sleep
so peacefully

How dare they
come with double
edged swords
on missions
to deceive

How dare they
scrutinize, oppose,
and speak lies upon me

How dare they
claim to be blood
but lead adversity

They say
"How dare you?"
as though it's me

They play the game so careful
to make people believe
that you are the
epitome of their grief
That you are the one
living wrongfully

How dare they
come like wolves
disguised as sheep
with their alibi
being that we are family

No.
My family doesn't
do those things
My family,
doesn't intentionally
cross me

My family doesn't
abuse me, use me
or ridicule me

My family doesn't
accuse me when
I'm speaking truthfully

Victimize me
for my transparency
Guilty consciences,
apparently
As though I spilled
their secrets carelessly
when I only
testified
my own stories
for God's glory

This isn't an attention scream
Crying for help wouldn't do a thing
unless I'm crying to the Lord

I've fought many lonely years
on the frontlines of these wars

Still bear the scars
on my heart

Still miss a beat
occasionally
when the pain hits deep
and the rhythm of peace
seems to escape me
Oh Lord, please save me

Some of them
I've even defended
regardless of circumstances

Was I just a fool for believing
that one day these people
would stop the deceiving
One day we would
possibly be friends
Relationships would be mended
Was it all just pretending,
over and over again?
Still the same old enemies
disguised as changed
then it's the same again

Same faces
Same lies
Same blaming me
for their lives
Still excusing their behaviors
Never givers, always takers

Same intentions to manipulate
everybody that I'm the
black seed planted
Deflection all the way
to hell's gates

I'm honestly
so sorry to say
that I might not
see y'all in heaven one day

How dare they
Father tell me
How dare they
think this is healthy
as though abuse is love
based on their rules
they made up

I'm trying to count my losses
cause' I don't play the game

Selling rumors
to those who bought it
Let God judge
their shame

One day,
they all will be living in misery
for the things they did to me
They don't want me to be free
from their satanic puppetry

Let it be, let it be
I'm trying Father
I need your Holy purity
to run through me like water
I want to make God proud
of His daughter

How dare they
think they have the authority
to control me, they don't own me

My steps are ordered
by the one who adores me,
supports me
Never puts me out
for their own profitability
of superficial investments
back into their pride at
humilities expenses

I did some things in my life
It's true I've never been perfect
but choices verses circumstances
are two different worlds

The Word says before swine
to never cast pearls
But I never realized
that in this world,
sometimes it's your own blood
that you have to keep your pearls from

Still I say,
how dare they

attempt to prosper weapons
against one of God's children

How dare Satan
think that I'm willing
to pass up my blessing
at the end of this lesson

In the name of Jesus
I dare them
to question God's power
to sentence
those without repentance
to His conviction

On the Judgment Day,
Father, who will forgive them?

Get Over Me

You can't hold my past against me
No you can't
Not sure who gave you permission
Are you some kind of salesman
getting paid by commission?
Are you earning bonus points while fishing
for any little bit of dirt you can find?
Well in case you didn't notice
I'm busy living my own life
So while I'm very flattered
that you take the time
to gossip to them behind my back
Perhaps you should recognize
those same folks talk about you
Don't be mad, just stating facts
They say we are the company we keep
So when you see me rolling with royalty
People washed by the blood of the true king
Walking around like a brand new me
and you're still talking about the things I used to be
or the few things you could dig up
for the sake of momentary popularity
As if you've been granted immunity
from being judged for your own way
I think you should take a minute to
rethink the things you say
before my name manages to
be the highlight of your day
Understand you have no authority
No control over me
So whether you do or don't support me
It doesn't change a thing
My destiny was written by an author
who created every living thing
I've inherited these blessings

and every promise He will keep
So how is it you think you're
so Godly, to hold my past against me
when even God has let it go
Like you're too holy for Jesus
but dirty working for those votes
I'm sure everybody will think you're cool in hell
and you'll have plenty of company
to comfort you as well
Because deflection is infectiously spreading
If y'all are so stuck on me
How can you face
your own reflections for long enough
to ever enter repentance for your sins?
Just some food for thought
while you are busy dishing out my business
and all that made up stuff you talk
I hope you can live with yourself
knowing you have a rotten heart
Serving no purpose at all
but to beat down others
While you have picked a lovely subject
I think that you should get over me
and get right with God
Every day is a chance
to change who you are.

Freedom Within

Naysayers keep nayin'
I don't live behind illusive paintings
Can't rewrite who I am
Brushes will soon burn
God be the judgment of what I deserve
Good things are coming, I feel it within
I'm not running, I'm elevating to freedom
These boxes, I don't need them
Your demons, I don't conceive them
Feel my heart? It's still beating
I'm not dead, I'm still speaking
Undefeated, still breathing
Ever changing is the Season
Continuance of life
Spirit hasn't weakened
Still moving toward the light
Not blinded by the lies
Truth seeker
Between the lines reader
Intuition on point
Flawless direction
Skip past the mental noise
See the true intention
Preventive measures of deception
Reputation unaffected
In case you didn't get the message
I'm free, wings spreading
Most high led in, pursuing my quest
Innocence been plead
Do no time for false charges
Keep talking, I keep rising
The sun kissed my cheek
Told me to keep shining
I'm timeless
Even if you killed me

I'd survive it
My physical vessel
is not the end of my journey
Spiritual realm worthy
Peace thirsty,
leave y'all war deprived
Love worthy
Keep your hatred if you like
Still inspired
Still writing
Still chosen
Still potent
Won't play broken
Been through real pain
You think I'm ghosting
Just watching you be played
by your own game
Blow out your own flame
as the air from my free breeze
wisps by the enemies
Try to breathe my energy,
leave your negativity warped
Deflection against me
Got my mirror, keep yours
Got my freedom within
Just watch me soar
You cannot imprison the vision
of a woman who knows
what she's living for.

LOVE THOUGHTS

I Need Love

When the pressure persists
Pushing to check off everything on my list
and every endeavor just doesn't go as I wished
When my passion is all that motivates me to live
On my knees thanking God for this lifelong gift
There are still those moments where I wish
I had him, his kiss, his touch, the feeling of love
Knowing he's there when my day was rough
I know his was too
I don't think there is
a whole lot I wouldn't do
to have him in my arms
Sometimes I don't think I can hold on any longer
I see why some settle for second best
They just can't take the loneliness
and although I'm not condoning
anything outside of God's plans

I know what it's like to not quite understand
why on earth this person
hasn't made their grand entrance
What could possibly be stalling him
from meeting me?
I know I've got to calm my emotions
A believer truly shouldn't sound this hopeless
One minute I'm on the scene spitting poems
The next I seem to be ghosting
Cause' sometimes I just need time
to be chosen, get to know Him
so that I can get to know him
I know there isn't a man who can clone him
God is still molding,
so that means we're still growing
to the place we need to be
for us to meet with hearts open
I know how easy it is
to get our hearts broken
Especially when we just be aimlessly eloping
Conditioned that we've got to
belong to someone
even if it won't last
I'd rather be the epitome
of what it is to be the other half
See what I need is love,
not just a moment that will pass.

Simplicity

In the midst of complexities... it's rather funny
I long for those simple things that do or don't, require money

Honestly, I just want to chill with you
over hot coffee or tea, whichever you prefer...

I know I seem like the kind of woman
who is hard to please
but I beg to differ...

Sure, I have standards as any woman should
Be truthful, be faithful, and don't bring me hurt
Be trustworthy, somebody who will never
underestimate my worth
Don't take me for granted
give me what I deserve
Don't say you're there,
then run for the hills
when things turn for the worst
Be by my side forever or not at all
I need a man with a brave heart

I guess that is too much to ask after all
or at least, for the average brother

But sugar, whoever, wherever, you are...
Whatever your name, your age, your career
or however much money you make...
Whether or not you've ever imagined
marrying a woman of my race
I trust God that you were especially made

Even if many have said
words that always leave me unsettled
that they just aren't on my level yet...

I know that the man for me will never
need to say those words

I know that there is a man who yearns
for the same simplicity
that makes my heart hit the curb

So many nights I feel like I'm crashing
took a wrong turn
Like I may never, ever... ever...
be found by my eternal lover

Oh baby, it hurts me so much
that you and I aren't here
to share these hot cocoa mugs
that we're not by the fire
talking about the simple stuff
That we haven't even shared
a few sentences as time
seems to be running up

I'm young, but I'm not getting younger
Tell me where is he, where is my eternal lover???

I'm speaking to the Lord
I'm crying out to God
It isn't healthy anymore
Please, send him on his way
and tell him not to stop

Keep going
Don't look back
You're so close
You're on the right track
I can feel you, moving toward me

You drive me crazy
I'm losing my mind
Where is my man to
carry these groceries
with me, help me
Share dinner
over candle lights

You know I didn't make these
love jam playlists just for myself
You know I don't write this poetry
just to be published,
in award winning books on a shelf

I don't really care what we're doing
as long as we aren't doing it alone

What I'd give to have you in the audience
watching me rock these microphones

What I'd give for us to have a home
start a family of our own...

I don't know who you've been with before
I don't know when you'll walk through those doors
I don't know if you've ever loved a woman
deep down to her core

But I know that you will never
love another woman more
then you will love me
Your complex queen, of sweet simplicity

I just want whatever each day brings
One step at a time

I want the birds to sing in the morning time
I want to find nests together in the trees
I want to lie on the grass together
Have a picnic, in the soft breeze

I want destiny between you and me
I want berries from the orchard
We pick them for our basket
A moment of simplicity
Another side of intimacy
I want you to share
all of your visions with me
However silly
However crazy

Whoever told you
the things you'd never be
I want to tell you
that you will

I want the simplicity
to ease those heavy hills
weighing you down
Who made you frown
Probably the same kind of fool
who has me hurting right now

But it's all good, we'll be fine
Soon you'll be in my hood... yes our paths will align...
For all you know, we're just on opposite ends

So if you meet me in the middle
just like an old friend
Reuniting again
whether we have, or haven't met

God knows the secrets
The mysteries
of you and me
From your rib,
He created a woman
for you to marry

Don't let them tell you
that this doesn't exist
You know what you felt
and heard from God's lips

He breathed me into your soul
So just breathe free, and you
will know which way to go

These may be some of
the simplest words
I've ever wrote

I dream of you and me
on a love boat
Maybe with rows
Sailing away together
Living the love notes
that some have written
but manifested, never

Let's live those simple memories
Let's be... those lovers on the beach

Let's kiss on the sea
on the ferry
that leads

to a private place
where we can go

Let's live a simple way
move with the flow
Let God and let go

Honey I know it's so hard
Living on the boulevard
of broken hearts
We're both scarred
We're damaged goods
But we're not worthless
just misunderstood

But if it brings you a little peace
Just rest your diary inside of me
I will hold onto your keys
Don't worry
Baby I'm sorry
for what they did to you and me
But you and I are beautifully
imperfect beings

Mentally
Emotionally
Spiritually
Physically

Anybody who tells you
that you need to be
alienated from humanity
just for the truth you speak

Trust me...
they don't know any better
But these days won't last forever

One day we will slow dance
in the heaven's above
One day our only romance
will be a spiritual love

So come... I'm waiting...
at the bottom step
to Heaven

You are the one that
keeps me stationed
patient... praying...
pressing...
Giving God my questions
Keeping faith
in Him to answer
Reserving my temple
for the day you take my hand
and I answer... I do...
Yes my love... I do...

I love you
It's simple
when it's true

It's simple
loving you

Simplicity
is all we'll ever need

Life is full of complexities
Last heart beats
Losing jobs and money

Complicated pregnancies
Healing from tragedies
Friends who become enemies
Families who disagree
Loved one's bringing adversity
Raising children, in this society
Figuring out our priorities
Trying our best to be
the best we can...

But all I want is simplicity
with my man
When all is said and done
Finally some silence
for you and I to enjoy

See I would give you a child
A girl or a boy
I would do anything
to see you smile
Anything, for you boy

You make me want to
remove every sin in me
You make me, want to continue
living a life of purity

You strengthen
the goodness in me
You change my maybes
to "Yes I believe!"

that God has for me
a king... a king of
sweet, simplicity

Yes darling...
Let's simply be
the manifestation
of those dreams

I know, you are
dreaming of me
This is, a two way street
that leads
to soul mates
who are ready
for love,
simply for eternity.

Brother of God

The thought of meeting him seems...
indescribable
But since I was born
with the scribe in me, here I go
Heart to soul,
he gives me faith when I've lost hope
When my past persuades me
"Don't believe in true love no more,"
no see, he makes all other
men evaporate from fantasy thoughts
Brother of God, you're all I want
Positioning myself for him
so I'm ready when he comes
Stepping mine up in more ways than one
Not only finish my degree,
publish books of poetry,
and release that album finally
But he makes me want to be,
the kind of wife he needs, a good thing indeed
and he sets me free from things
other brothers did to me
He brings me joy
when I could cry myself to sleep
I know this sounds sweet
like an ordinary love piece
but this is something deep,
see I'm hearing God speak
Please do attempt to tell me differently
I'm not even slightly entertained by disbelief
when I tell you there is a man just for me
This mustard seed is about to be a tree
Yes I'm waiting for the man who will marry me
So consider my body, his territory
created for him to worship
To God be the glory,

when the days I fornicated have ended
Thinking of him, frees me from sin
When temptation has me lusting,
I'm reminded to be patient for him
See there is nothing like a true brother of God
Lord he's all I want, please send him my way soon
Made changes in my life, some may not understand
all for the promise of having that man
so you'd be out your mind, to think
I'll sacrifice eternity just for one night
when the man who deserves me
is coming right on time
Yes that brother of God is all mine
And on the day he lays eyes,
he will know I'm his wife
Crazy as that may sound
In my brother of God,
I have no doubts
when God told me,
He is leading him to me now.

A Good Thing

He said, one day I'll make a good mother
a good wife, and a good friend
He said he was in so much amazement
with my maturity, but I told him
Brother don't reward me
for the things they lack
The minimum is no exception
I'm just living with true tact
Nobody forced me to sign some contract
but if God says it shall be
then from these ego chains I'll release
Obedience is not an option,
but to those who disbelieve
I hope they realize,
everything isn't what it seems
Time is not a guarantee
Salvation is not owed to you or me
But I thanked him,
for he meant well in the things he said to me
Excuse me if I be too deep,
but I don't know any different
I don't see myself in some supernatural position
I'm only a decent human being
Striving, struggling, to break free, repeatedly
from these traps set by our society
But I don't practice sobriety, it comes naturally
My writing is my high to me,
for there I have no gravity
and brother I have learned
that here on earth, the way this system works
with freedom of expression,
we must expect the worst
Suppose the truth about them
is found within your words
Suppose you be testing,

the very thing they deem their worth
Surfacing their pain to a healing place
Suddenly, you are the one to blame
when the true oppressor now is self
Yes we're digging our own graves
Living behind tombs, long before our death
If I tell you I'm in love with you,
Brother would you lose your breath?
Have you ever experienced,
this type of affection yet?
Do you, find me divine,
because I'm affectionate?
Does my non-repressing chest,
scratch that spot that hasn't itched yet?
Baby don't you see...
I'm only being the woman God wants me to be
so if I walk the extra mile, what will you think?
Would it make me seem like I'm going
through temporary insanity?
Have the conditioned majority branded me
based on the boxes of acceptance
Is the reason you adore me
because you can no longer stand them?
Have you too been abandoned,
for your self-defining standard
But I see you're still standing,
so your prayers have too been answered
Now answer...
Has your anointing
ever caused sick people to feel poisoned?
Do they run from the cure your words have to offer?
Has anyone ever told you, you're a good father?
No doubt in my mind,
you're raising him to be a prince of prophecy
There is no surprise to me you see the God in me

For you my brother, are not diseased by deflection
but rather you look at me, deeply reflecting
I want to be your best friend, but it's so much more
With or without those compliments
I can feel your warmth
and even if we were born
in two separate places
I feel we're connected, spiritually adjacent
Yes I enjoy our conversation
but your energy is communicating
I am completely taken
You've broken me way in
If ever I come out again
Remind me of all the ways that you refine me
How you've helped to change and redesign me
just by being there beside me
And if I don't take enough credibility
for being all of these good things
Please don't think I'm being rude
I just am so tired of the things people do
and every time they do something good
They want everyone to honor them
when we should be doing so much more
Not looking for superficial reward
We are not superior nor were we ever pure
We were put here to be servants to the Lord
so who should mop this floor we all stand upon?
Are we all too busy looking for glass houses
with pockets full of rocks?
Who called war in the middle of me praising God?
Some people think this is what they want,
But on the judgment day
Oh, on the judgment day
I often wonder to myself,
what everyone will say

Do they think it's all a game safe enough to play
A good God he is, but a fool he ain't
I've never been perfect
but I'm honest with my mistakes
Perfection I won't claim but
every day I make progression to better my way
What a relief it is to find a man who does the same
Speaking with him for ten minutes equates
to a lifetime of the average dialog
He always supplies, food for thought
He doesn't buy the rumors they bought
just because they're being sold
You know he's a man by the way he walks
with the holy spirit in his soul
If ever he got lost I'd help him find his way home
Here in my arms, there resides an unconditional love
he finds irresistible and him being mine is considerable
but for now, we'll just grow, evenly yoke
Mystery the future holds, but that's alright
With me, trust the destiny been sown
to be a good thing
He said one day, God will send me a husband
I looked at him with eyes that said
"Who told you he hasn't?"

Love Could Come Sooner

Love sure could come sooner, on a night like tonight
Come on, somebody out there has got to testify
Feel a woman wishing she could, move the clock
forward and backward, all at the same time
See it all goes by too fast as it is
but if I could just bump into him
You know what I'm talking about
Do I have to spell the words out my mouth?
I'm waiting for the man to father my first child
I'm waiting for a bed that will be undefiled
I'm not looking for him, those days are over now
but I'm half-wishing he would hurry up, get molded now
Sometimes it's all too simple, being single
You miss the cuddling a little
Sitting by the window,
daydreaming he would come to your rescue
Sure there are men who can almost tempt you
but if it isn't the man God sent you
It just doesn't hold your interest
for more than a few minutes
I'm out here handling my business
but who is there for me when the day is finished?
Just me myself and I
While that's alright,
I know this isn't all there is to life
As much as we be on that independent hype
Every woman needs a man and
every man needs a wife
so I'm holding on
with all my might
I'm trying to stay chill
but you can see it in my eyes
Something is missing on the inside
I know he will be seeking me in due time
but love could come a little sooner

on a night like tonight
when I'm sensitive but don't want to cry
He's got the medicine to make me alright
Been waiting for my cure for a long time
Don't want to settle for an urge
when I can have a lifetime
of making love with a man who's all mine
Even though this guy, and that guy, are so fine
They aren't the guy designed with me in mind
Even though sometimes I wonder if I'm wasting time
Missing out on options I let pass me by
But that's just the flesh and spirit fight
Although love could come sooner
on a night like tonight
I must put my trust
in the true hands of time.

SLIPPING

Irony of the Situation

It's the irony of the situation
that you would leave me so complacent
with these silly expectations
Love making, vacating, babies incubating
Well it's kind of fun isn't it, exploring the idea
Like we had no fear but we had no idea
that wishful thinking could appear
as true manifestation
So we stayed drunk on liquid conversation
Debating about everything from
top five emcees to fornication
but we didn't really see the risk to be taken
if somebody caught feelings in this relation
And of course, it had to be you
No wait, it had to be me
Long distance love has never been my cup of tea
No matter how much sugar we add to this thing

Baby, it's just too sweet to be
Needlessly, you fiend for me
Lay to sleep, dream of me
I try to say it's a one way street,
then I ask do you miss me
Such hypocrisy, forgive me
Thought I was rolling indie,
but you want to roll with me,
and either I'm too flattered to let it go,
or we dealing real matters of the heart and soul
Tell me what it be, what you see, looking at me
to be so adamant about being my king
But it's like come on baby,
neither one of us are in the position
to change our way of living
Two separate coasts,
already sound like love imprisoned,
Hearts grow fonder until they grow sour
Wyclef & Mary warned us about this kind of love
Do you need a reminder, this can be dangerous
Just as I get to saying, you bring more irony to the situation
Claiming, you're supposedly over me
but two days later you're obsessively phoning me
Missing me terribly, want to be holding me
Noticeably, you and me,
are lost in a sea of promises we can never keep
No, no before you speak,
promise me it's not what I think
You've fallen deeply in.... no this couldn't be
Our situation don't need no more irony
This love hit us both violently, cause' it's all black and blue
Swollen inside, my heart aches for you and you for I
Yet ironically I seem to find every reason why
I've got to say goodbye
Sometimes we even fight when you come to town

Cause' I be fronting, I be giving you the run around
only to find us touching down anyhow
And that's the irony of the situation
I say no to one sip
then next thing I know I'm wasted
off of, irony on the rocks
Don't take advantage of me
when I'm as weak as you are
Seeing stars, room spinning, can't walk, blurry vision
These are all of the symptoms of our ironic addiction
I tell him to stop but he just keeps drinking
and then I drink him, and we're falling all over again
Yes that's the irony, of the situation.

Tempted

I should go home
but I enjoy being here with you
I shouldn't be in this room
but baby, the things I'd do
to make all of your dreams
come true in these minutes
If I could just fall in love
with you at this instance
Show you the difference,
before it's all too late
Show you those women,
who've helped condition your way
to the point where the real thing
begins to intimidate
You don't know
if you should love me or run away
but then when I get up to leave,
you tell me I really should stay
I'm putting back on all of my clothes,
before babies get made
Oh trust me they would
Trust me I would love you that good
Have you fantasizing about
life beats inside me while you're inside me
Feeling my heart beat trying to fight me
to keep up with this passion
I really would love to put these words into action
but this spirit and flesh war I'm having
You have me battling, it's time to go home
But since you've been asking
thought I'd let you know, no!
I wouldn't disappear
If you were for real, I'd be here
Yes if I was your woman...
I'd take your last name

and let the whole world hear
I'm in love with this man
on his knees with my hand
Put that ring on me if you understand
Marriage is more than just a white show
It's confirmation of the eternal binding
between two souls
And yes, I would travel the distance
just to give you a bouquet of kisses
And yes if I knew I could get away with this
without doing damage
I'd lay down in that bed with you shameless
as past faces vanished
I'd take you to so many places
you've never been
Show you life on other planets,
slow dance on the moon
You'd be getting homesick
whenever I'm not with you
Home is where the heart is
and my love is the roots
There isn't a woman on this earth
who could love you the way I will
if you don't let me get up out of here right now
before it's all too late
Type of love make a man travel
in and out of state
Make you go near insane
when I'm not around
I think you should probably
walk me to my car right now
before you end up being
the father to my first child
Do you hear what I'm saying,
darling I'm not playing

This isn't the ordinary kind of love
you've been making
This stuff would have our chests aching
in contemplation
of how we would make it
when the distance begins to kick in
Baby stop playing, you know what this is
This the kind of love
that would have us on a hit list
from the jealousy people would get
when they see the way you
loving me, so passionate
Got nerve to be asking me
why I'm panicking, to get dressed
Do you know how close I am getting
to just doing it
I'm not running from you,
I'm running from me
Falling in love with you,
every second I let escape me
Please let me leave, baby just stop
Why can't you see,
this is not about what I want
It's about what I need,
not about what we've got
Just let me get my keys
before I do something you'll never forget
Make a grown man go crazy
without a single regret
You'll be chasing me around
just to confess that you love me
No you can't love me just yet!
How could love be so ruthless?
Like it just don't care when or where
Show up when it will,

don't even ring the door bell
This just isn't fair with the way that we feel
that I've got to walk out this door
But I promise you,
this love will be worth waiting for.

Two Steps Back

Unlighted Candles
Unset the Pandora channel
Refasten my bra
Retighten your tie
Zip up your jeans
Unmake our love
Take back the Red Snapper
Plantains, rice, & vegetables
from the Jamaican spot
and please change back
all the clocks
The night I met you
at your church
after I performed
I thought we were just
networking
until the next weekend
Oh my God.
Please take back the phone call
Give me a busy signal
Forget that all night long talk
before our abstinence was sabotaged
Send back the invitation for me to
rest my head at your spot
after lunch when I was
too tired to drive back
Put the T-Shirt back in the drawer
Why did you let me get comfortable?
Should have kept my church clothes on
Brother may I, take two steps back
All of those feelings,
can you just not catch?
Incense back in the box
Put your pants back on
You never got in my car

I never drove to your house
I never stole your heart
wearing nothing but my crown
Un-name me your angel,
you've finally found
I just don't think I'm ready now
Fold back up the shower towel
You never showed me how to
run the hot water
or change the temperatures
I never ever cried in your arms
after my temple had me delivered
You never asked me if I'm falling in love
after you told me you were
and I told you I wouldn't know
even if I was, because
every time I thought
this was the one, it never was
So if this is,
whether I know it or not
may be irrelevant
Oh please just....
take away your kiss, separate our lips
pretend you never saw me naked
Pretend we never gave in to our flesh
justified by dynamics, like the connection
neither of us could resist
Cancel the first text message I sent
Stop my finger from hitting send
Better yet, don't reply
Deny your attraction to me,
like I'm not your type
Oh my... I am, aren't I?
Did he just say, keys to his house?
Were those my key words, to get the hell out?

I'm just not used to this, why is he doing this?
Why is he treating me like I'm his perfect fit?
Why does he favor all of my flaws?
Why is he opening up his heart?
There must be a catch, I await the applause
This is just a reality TV show right?
This is all scripted and those lines memorized
Undo that mesmerized look in his eyes
Take two steps back
Let's redo everything the way we should have
or just, never do any of it at all
as if I had never given you my number
because I didn't have business cards
Lord this man is divorced
and has a daughter
with a jealous ex-wife who
doesn't want him to move on!
Clearly this can't be what I want
and I'm not ready for this to be what I need
He says he wants to be good to me
but I think he's a tad bit too old for me
This can't be the man you've molded for me
Why does he have to understand me?
Why can't he find me complicated like the rest?
Why is he perfectly content with me
going back to abstinence after we've already had sex
He was supposed to get quiet and run away
He was supposed to go back to his old lifestyle
and play the game so I could say
he's a dog, and I'm moving on
But he told me to follow my heart
and listen to God
that if he's been practicing
for nine months before us
then he can hold on

Oh no...
Let go
Don't tell me you're okay
with us taking things slow
Disagree with me so I can make this easy
You don't really need me
You need... somebody your own age
I'm an artist,
this lifestyle will be too crazy
for your laid back ways
Right now it all seems okay but surely
the insecurities are on their way
But you say
you're okay with my dreams
You just want to be a part of me
You want to see me reach stardom and be happy
You say, I'm all the woman
to keep your spark lit
You know where your heart is
Prayed for me to come and I did
I don't believe it, take two steps back
Stay at a distance, so I can forget that
feeling of having you close to me
Forget that I ever read you poetry
between the sheets, lying next to me
Feeling stronger for me, with each word I speak
You can't love me, you just love my body
You must be just like the others who wronged me
Unmake those promises to me
Tell me a lie and quit with all of this honesty
Give me a reason to walk away from you and me
But you tell me you'll always be there
You ask me if this is one of those things
where I just disappear
and usually that'd be a question I'd ask

so it sounds different from here
How many mixed messages must I deliver
before you get tired of my fear
Why did you ever kiss away my tears?
You should have let them fall
Let me cry alone
because that is all I've ever known
So why are you still here?
Don't you have somewhere to go?
How long will it take for your true colors to show?
I'm taking two steps back because I don't know
if this is that real stuff or you just feel lust
Praying to God to remove him if he isn't the one
Remove him at once if he's not my husband
If he's not the father to my first born
If he's just here to break my heart in the future
If he won't be faithful if he won't be true
Show me the rest of the steps when I take two
Help me walk away from him when my flesh a fool
Reveal the truth, about this man trying to
exclusively take me as his woman
Undo our hands and the chemical ties
and we can just go on with our lives
Lord help me make up my mind
before I take two steps back
If I can take two,
I can take two more after that
I'll never look back
So before I break this man's heart
Show me his purpose on my path
because I'm on the verge of calling
this whole thing off
before it ever had a chance to last
Maybe it all moved too fast
Didn't I used to like it like that?

Why do I keep two-stepping back
but yet I'm still in the presence of this man
playing them Neo soul tracks
Those are all of my songs
Please let something I don't like come on
Oh, My God...
Candles, music, getting hot
Make it stop
Freeze us there in that moment
right before he ate me up like I wanted
Still want it, can't have it
It's time to be strong
Time to take two steps back
until I get an answer from God
and accept we can't take back
what has already been done
So the ultimate challenge has come
to know love for love, sex aside
But I don't want to know his love
if it won't last a lifetime
So let me pass this test
with someone who is meant to be mine
I promise I can handle it,
if he's just not that guy
One step at a time
But if it is him
Please Lord,
open my eyes.

One Week

I haven't seen you in one week
and you've asked me, "Do you miss me?"
but I don't know what to say back
I'm having trouble grasping the emotion to express that
I hope I don't sound selfish
or come off like a sign that reads "No Trespass"
and I know if I did you would respect that
but I just don't know if you're the man for me yet so
I think I need time to just do me again
before I stick myself somewhere I don't belong
I can tell this kind of love would go hard
Now I know that's what a woman like me wants
but there are some things I need
before I go getting married
Truthfully, I want to live separately
Have my own space,
instead of moving into your place right away
Now I know you're talking that key talk,
but I'm having these thoughts
I need to do like Jill Scott and take "A Long Walk",
as I meditate with God,
I'm drifting away from this thing you say we are
but then I begin to think about it
and I miss you after all
I'm happy you called,
so please don't get confused by my restless heart
tossing & turning in different directions
Baby I'm sorry if this is hurting you,
please don't stress it
If you're meant for me then
even this moment is meant to be
If you're not,
then I wish you happiness with somebody
Honestly, either way is cool with me
Whatever it will be

I don't expect a commitment
just because we became one
between the sheets
This doesn't mean you're the man who will
fall in love with me
even though you say you are
I can't take man's word
without my prayers being answered
I can't just give it all to you
at the drop of a dime
I can't change my single status
when it would be a lie
if I haven't made up my mind
My love, you don't have to cry
I know that real men do
I don't intend to leave you feeling blue
however I can no longer be superwoman
coming to another brothers rescue
I just want to be my own woman
without the potential for another heart break
to come between my dreams
See I'm trying to focus on a lot of things
so tell me where would I even find the energy
But you say I wouldn't have to worry
You say, you're not in a hurry
You say you'd never hurt me
Words I want so badly to believe
I don't even hold your past
against the reborn man you claim to be
but I'm just trying to figure out
if this juice is worth the squeeze
Please bear with me, I'm not crazy
I'm just a little scared to be your lady
and I'm not quite ready to close the option window
I feel like our exclusivity may have to wait a little

Even though I won't be sleeping with nobody
This doesn't mean that it's because of you and me
It's just a personal choice I've made for the time being
I don't know long it is going be
Maybe I'll wait for a man to get down on his knee
Maybe I can be a stronger woman than I used to be
If you think there is any possibility
that you aren't going to be able to hold out for me
It's probably best you leave
Don't wait around for me
But you said that your queen of the nest is me
You said you can take the good and the ugly
While all of that is sweet,
we can say a lot of things, so we'll see
what will be revealed to me
I don't want you to stop feeling me
Just keep it real with me
Am I too much to take?
Are you bothered by the fact that
I cannot say yes and I cannot say no
I'm not used to this predicament
because I used to force love to grow
Now I'm just absorbing the natural cycle
Eventually there will be a reality enclosed
in the envelopes of our souls
I don't just want to love the idea of loving you
All of this is brand new here
I'm just telling you the truth,
There are plenty of things I still
don't know about you, and you about me
so we can't be so quick to dive into that sea
I feel like we skipped to chapter five in just one week
I've learned in the past how dangerous this can be
I'm thankful that you've taken two steps back with me
but I'm not going to sell you any dreams

like tell you it will always be you and me
when I don't know where it all will lead
so please don't make this harder than it has to be
The best thing for us to do is let God speak
and if we really are destiny,
please forgive me for my humanity
If you see something I can't yet see
know that He will instill the sight in me
Don't give up on me if you know it before me
but we can't just jump the gun,
when it's only been one week.

Do You!

Maybe I owe you something like an apology
I know it's not always an easy thing to say sorry
but I realize, I... kind of led you on just a bit
I realize men have feelings too but this wasn't my intent
Now I don't underestimate your intelligence
nor do I misjudge your relationship with God
You truly believe it in your heart,
that I'm the angel you prayed for
but I am not an angel that's for sure
yeah I'm a good woman but... I make mistakes
and giving into my flesh with you was one I made
We hadn't even been on that many dates
I mean really, what were we thinking?
Now you're asking me for reasons
why this just can't work
Well right now,
I just need my freedom
to heal from lots of hurt
Spread my wings out, learn how to fly again
God gave me a new pair now,
but my heart
is still under construction
I don't have time to think about,
all of these other assumptions
This doesn't have anything to do with a man
so you want me to come up with an explanation
if that isn't the case
Okay....
I prayed for God
to take you away if this isn't real
That's when I saw us drift apart, so far
Don't say you didn't feel the shift of heart
But you say I'm the one who's got it twisted
on some God is sending us mixed messages
Well, I don't serve a God of deception

So please don't use our faith to get up in my face
I've got enough going on for the two of us
Would you rather a lie? Look you in your eyes...
tell you I'm in love, well that I just can't do
See a year ago, I may have settled for you
Said to myself,
soon as a good man come, it's a wrap!
But when I learned that good men
really aren't as scarce as women act
I realized, he can be a good man
but that doesn't mean he's good for me
Please understand it's even bigger than
just being treated like a queen
It's about being with the man destined for me
As much as you may think I'm missing out
Really I'm just saving us both time right now
So that we don't have to find out three years down
that it just isn't working out
Either way, I'm sorry you are hurting now
but you can't just force love to sprout
See I've got to stand my ground
This doesn't mean I'm not sincere
in apologizing for the rain cloud
Trust me, it would have been much worse
if I let it prolong
I know the idea of new love lost hurts,
but why does it have to be a loss?
There's a blessing in every lesson,
if you can see the gain
The nice things you did for me,
I do appreciate
Why can't we both just blame it on fate?
Walk away without a sour taste
Chips in the shoulder when we cross paths
I should have never come over

Let's leave it at that
We can't go back, and you know it took two
So I'm going to get back to doing me
and you can do you.

Forgive Me Father

Undeniably a sinner,
I stand before you with a testimony
Most of all I testify for the brief time
when I didn't even feel guilty at all
Truthfully, the only reason I felt guilty
was because I didn't
but I knew the lightening would strike my womb
and I would drop to my knees beneath the king
I would praise your throne and say
"Jesus I'm Sorry!"
But you see,
I didn't give God the glory
when the sun was still shining
Selfishly waited for the rain to start pouring
before I could enter repentance
That was about the time that Tabitha showed up
and then the Lord Spoke
He put Tabitha to rest and made my spirit
rise up to his hold, and he held
I looked him right in the eyes and he told, and I fell
Crying the most painful cry from my soul and I felt
the punishment for the piece of temple, I did sell... for free
like I just let a man pick me from the menu and fornicate me
I am guilty as charged, so I wished the old me well
and prayed for my new heart
Oh Lord, this is going to be hard... isn't it?
This is going to be a long walk, with a lot of limps in it
I'm going to make mistakes and sometimes
I'm going to ask,
"God why? God how,
can I make it through another day?"
The Devil is going to keep on trying to send me astray
I'm going to give into temptations
every now and then even if I'm saved
because my flesh is weak

like any woman's, like any man's
My ever erupting sexuality has deceived me
during times when I couldn't just turn to God's hands
I wanted a man to love me
I wanted a man to kiss me
I wanted a man to lay naked with me
rock me to sleep and call me baby
but I wasn't ready for the morning time to come
when I was just another sheep
who forgot to praise thy
But now, I'd rather have a man
who can pray me up than lay me up
Lord I've had enough with all of this being tough
Breaking down in dark corners on my own time
Even during the times
when they witness this daughter cry
I've never completely let it go
I'm sick of this defense mechanism in front of people
I'm sick of bottling it all in
until I overdose, nodding off on the pain
I let saturate for one too many days
Forgive me Father for my, flesh-like ways
Forgive me for repressing my spirit
and not expressing faith
Forgive them for tampering
with my persevering but make them pay
For this price, doesn't go one way
And the truth is,
we'd all probably be in debt
if you really gave us what we deserved
for the sins we repent
And the truth is I'm probably going to
do more stupid things that make me praise Jesus
when it hurts but doesn't kill me in the end
Some people say they are grown

but I say that I am growing
Some people think that they know,
but the day cometh when he will show them
I'm just hoping I can open myself to you like Jesus' wounds
I'm hoping you can learn to love all of my imperfections
I heard a voice saying, "I already do,"
looking in the visor mirror but it's just me
There is nobody else in here, so it must be
The same voice says "Trust me,"
I cry out to the Lord, "I need a husband to love me!"
but the Lord is jealous and tells me,
"First, you must love me!"
and there I was, the good, the bad, and the ugly
Beautiful by the reflection but
even I've got stuff up my sleeve
so I pray, Lord please cleanse me
I've had enough of me!
I want to be more than who I want to be
I want to be who you need me to be
Now I have found the God in me,
but I need you to teach me how to work this machine
You can let them judge me because they too will be
The fact is most of them are here
because they've committed triple the sins as me
But that don't make me no better right here and now
Lord, you have a right to expect more out of your child
but you know I've been less
because you know all of my filthy secrets
Still you fill me with an angelic glow,
as my hands raise to the ceiling
If there is nobody out there in the world
who knows what I'm feeling
You do, you knew
tonight I'd attend
not one worship service, but two

Then I'd finally find the time
to sit down and speak with you
Tell you what you already know I've done
but I'm the one you need to hear it from
Forgive me Father, I'm sorry
Forgive me Father, I've forsaken thy
Thank you Father, for breaking me
just to build me up
the way you want me to be, spiritually
because the flesh of humanity,
will never know how to honor our king
Forgive me Father for the temporary insanity
when I thought lust was love and gave in
Lied to myself just for
the confirmation of rationalization
Well yesterday I was praying
but right now I'm praising
I thank Him because we've all shamed him
Don't tell me what you are or you ain't
because you are when you are put in that situation
You are no more the perfect saint than I've been
Lord knows who I've been and where I am going
So if this heart is breaking, let there be no complaining
Regardless of the pain I'm in, it is better than Satan
Lord sweep away the pieces and give me another
One that will not be so weakened by the skin of a brother
Teach me how to be a wife, and a mother
Prepare me, for the man
you've planned to be my lover
Make me stop and think next time
Show me how to break free,
let me be your butterfly
Not mistaken my thighs for wings,
when it feels so right
Father, this is my testimony

Please forgive me tonight
With my new heart,
please give me a new mind
so I can see with new eyes,
clarity during confusion
My body is not for their charity
It is to be worshiped
I know this, but still Father,
I've been foolish
Now you I will honor,
through this process of deliverance.

MY CELIBACY

Flesh

Flesh tugging at my spirit still
but now I have a stronger will so I can chill
Even though sometimes
those lines could be crossed, for real
I'm only human so you, probably know the deal
Liar I would be if I told you this was easy
Occasionally those temptations still deceive me
but the difference be, that they don't defeat me
A couple close calls
Sometimes I stumble then withdraw
On some, get up off, before we make lust
Clearly this isn't making love, if we aren't in, love
and even if we was, fornicating all the same
I'm still getting used to this whole life change
Now don't make it hard on a sister
trying to do the right thing
with all these thoughts in my brain

Like just do it and repent at church on Sunday
No I won't use His glory as my crutch
But sometimes it comes like a bug,
tricking me into thinking this is healthy
Telling me to just give in to the chemistry
That would be the enemy, messing me
Brother, stop caressing me
See I don't even want to be 'wifey',
I want the real thing
Why do we need a Y after the E,
to ease responsibility?
These men want all the goodies
without the ring
and for some women
that seems to be the in thing
but that's not for me
So before I slip into that category
Before I start telling you I'm sorry
Apologizing for the fact that,
I won't be hypnotized by this chemical trap
Explaining myself to a man in the heat of his flesh
Getting my keys from the nightstand
would be my best bet
Actions speak louder than words so,
I'm pretty sure you heard the message
when I went the opposite direction
I had to see past our connection
so I could see the sign telling me to stop
before I run that red light
Though my body said green, my spirit disagrees
creating this tension in me until I finally get up and leave
See my flesh be, tugging at my spirit still
but now I have a stronger will, so I can chill.

Intentional Temptations

It's kind of like you don't really hear me
when I explain where I'm at with my life
It's like you think that this is just a show
Like behind the scenes I'm still down for the ride
But in due time you will learn, this is for real
While fleshly desires may still burn,
God's spirit keeps me sealed
Stop trying to catch me at just the right time
If you love me, you should respect me
Stop tempting my mind
when you know some books have been closed
New chapters are in the mold
but you seem to believe that you can re-sculpt
as if you're in control
with your intentional temptations
spilling in between the pages
Hoping I'll eventually lose patience
Let you taste again
Trying to come at me with the things
that you knew were my favorite
It's like you don't care about my celibacy
or the way I am changing
In fact you'd probably prefer for me
to be how I was before
As long as it means sharing intimacy
with you behind closed doors
But you need to know that it's not yours
Your intentional temptations
have me at war no more with my flesh
I'm a grown woman now
I can keep my hormones in check
Just for the record
So quit with the pressure
As a matter of fact, keep it up
I'm just getting stronger

The soul ties have been cut
but you think my bed sheets
are the way back into my heart
Intentionally trying to tempt me
to let down all of my walls
See if you really loved me,
you'd stand by me on this walk
All of this just makes me see
that you are not my man of God
You probably think I'm just trippin'
or I'm temporarily a Christian
going through some phase
when I've always been
I just had not yet been saved
So please go away with your,
intentional temptations
Sex isn't selling me today
I'm no longer addicted
to your warm embrace
Yet every time lust tries to visit,
it always seems to be your face.

Waiting for Him

That night,
as my feet traveled miles
down a soft sand beach
Each wave that gently
stroked me delicately
made me think
about the way
making love should be

And I remember the moon
How she smiled at me
stretching her glow out
in arms reach
with a silver cup
to catch my tears
from dreams of love

I supposed that this was
what stars were made of
Nurtured like baby birds
by the glittery desires of
a maiden who has learned
that putting your hand in
an oven like Saturn will burn

But in a world of ugly secrets
It's easy for a girl
to mistake it for Venus
when we've seemingly arrived
at our destination

The shells understand me
when they find themselves
tucked in places they've never been

and then someone comes along
to take them, but do they ever listen?

Have you ever
held those shells
up to your ears,
and felt more connected
to the universe
then you'd been in years?

Just by hearing the heartbeat
of waves that have already passed
I wonder why we're always
concentrating on the past

But it was hard not to look back
when I saw two lovers hidden
where nobody could see them but me
and automatically I thought about
the we that used to be
and there was a part of me
that wondered...

I wondered if she
was rushing intimacy
there on that beach
because she was
afraid that he would leave
if she didn't give it up
In a society where,
there will always be
females optionally
who will open their
legs, to any old body

I'm sorry that they don't
love themselves enough
But I'm even sorrier
that these men fall for that stuff
and miss out on real love

I wanted to believe
that she loved he
and he loved she
That they were newly weds
celebrating being married

But it was funny cause'
when the moon dust
highlighted their hands in motion
I didn't see any rings shining
as he cracked her wide opened

Still I was hoping
for the sake of love
that her heart wouldn't be broken
when this was all done...
Because mine was,
even when I didn't make love

I held out, took my time
wanted a man to earn my trust
for just once... earn my love
Go the extra mile, to acknowledge
a woman's worth and such
But its funny cause'
It didn't seem to matter
even though it does

But the ironic part was
that for a moment I had
this really stupid thought

that maybe it was just
all my fault after all
How could I expect
a brother, to wait
to make love
When this was the walk
to which I was called
But then I paused...
Found myself caught
in the middle of a sand castle
washed over just as I was getting lost
It was there like a sign in the fog
Reminding me that I was royal after all

And just like the sand
goes with the ocean
in the way that it does
I need a man who goes with
my flow and knows his role
like nature loves

In a way unforced
that found me there
on that shore
Nobody told me
what to do when I got there
but somehow I just knew
what I was there to do

I was there to let loose
every single message
from every bottle of my soul
Go through every emotion
that I've repressed
when I was too scared, to let go

It was time,
to find a new shell
and get rid of the old
It was time,
to let the treasure map
I used to know, float
because that one
only led to fool's gold
It was time,
to be freed from
the strongholds
that deter me so

In my mind,
there have always been
some things
I didn't want to know
Being smart,
and intuitively gifted
are blessings indeed

But there were times
when I just didn't
want to have these prophecies
because being naive
was much more sweet
then the things
that I could see, spiritually

I can feel it, quite clearly
Not to mention
I've always been
a woman to observe
To listen...
To watch...

and I remember
Everything I've heard
Like puzzles,
pieces form together
and create a picture
Like the ones that broke my heart

But it's time to
throw these pictures in the sea
with all the love letters
that promised forever
until the ties were severed

It's time to allow myself
the pleasure to say
Real love,
I will wait for you
I am waiting
I know you are waiting too

It's time to lay here in my skin
with no manmade rules
and listen to the sounds of love
from an oceanic musical

I'm waiting for someone
to make me feel
like these songs do

As my ankles
submit to the tide
crashing into their skin
I'm somehow transitioned
into a paradise
where I am waiting for him
to come find his wife.

The Sixth Month of Celibacy

Okay... it's not easy
but it's better than HIV
It's better than an unwanted pregnancy
and it's a hell of a lot better than playing 'wifey'
to some guy who will never wife me
I'm getting kind of sick
of people treating this life change like a disease
Perhaps those would be the same individuals
who have actually contracted one
While I wouldn't pray that upon even my enemies
It's just a little crazy when I have to explain
why you just cannot have sex with me
And regarding when I plan
on reentering the dating scene... I don't
I plan on actually waiting
for the man God will send to me
I am sick of you looking at me like
I'm playing make believe
strung out on Cinderella fairy tales
when I tell you that I really do believe
that there is a man just for me
for whom I'll lift that wedding veil
There is no better process of elimination
then literally removing your tail, from the chase
Making it clear that you are not selling a bit
of what's between your legs
because you have been celibate for
one hundred sixty something days
I don't really understand why you are so amazed
Okay so I wasn't exactly the good girl before
and this wouldn't be the first time,
I've battled the celibacy war
It's just this time, I've chosen more wisely
It's not to rub it in your face
that together we won't be sleeping

Please stop making this all about you
when this is between me
and my relationship with God
If you expect me to be sorry, I'm not
If you think I've lost my mind then call me crazy
but the man for me won't be complaining
If you expect me to trade in my celibacy card
so that you can sex your way into my heart
You should probably consult with the nearest booty call
because however fine you are, you aren't fine enough
for me to lose out on real love for a little lust
Still I'm well aware of the challenges that will come
when celibacy for six months isn't that long
Some fellas may say no woman is that strong
to resist the right move at just the right time
Maybe they're right, which is why I pray to God
for peace of mind, otherwise I might
be snuggled up with some guy
See I'm celibate but I'm still alive
so yes there are times when
fornicating crosses my mind
but there are starting to be less of them
and more thoughts of being the right man's wife
on this sixth month of celibacy
defining a higher purpose in my life.

Withdrawal

We've all been plagued by some sort of addiction
but sometimes don't realize we were addicted
until we no longer give in
and on a night like tonight,
I really feel like sinning
Got that Jezebel spirit in my toes
but instead I'm here at home telling God
the things He knows
The thoughts that I think
when my hormones lose control
The thirst for affection, from a body so close
Nine months into celibacy and I'm still capable
of slipping up, relapsing,
giving up just to feel that passion
But the difference between now and then
lies within my actions and my awareness of
when I'm lacking the willpower to say no
See people forget, God holds the power to my soul
Just because I'm saved, doesn't mean I can't fall short
It doesn't mean my fantasies don't sometimes take over
or I don't consider dialing that number
or, answering that call
Sinning on Saturday and
going to church on Sunday to praise God
Just because I'm a saved woman
doesn't mean I don't have wants that feel like needs
So who am I to judge the fiend?
Doesn't everybody have their 'drug',
or thing that makes them weak?
So if making love is the thing I fight spiritually
Does that give anyone the right to judge me?
But see, I'm not even talking about
just sleeping with any old body
What about that one who I know still loves me?
or that other brother who was good to me

See you can still have standards and be living sinfully
So I get down on my knees and continue to speak
God please send that man of God to me
Don't know how much longer I can maintain my celibacy
You say it'd be better to be married than to live immorally
and I made the choice to wait for the one you have for me
Sometimes I'm good while I'm awake
and then I live it out inside my dreams
Lust attacking me, subconsciously
but I don't want you to be displeased
so please help me during these moments of withdrawal
when I'm feeling so sensual, and my flesh has me drugged
I wouldn't have even made it this long
if it wasn't for you, keeping me, this strong
Even if I know, it's wrong, it still feels so right
Sometimes my mind still blurs the lines
Did I think that this was love?
Oh God, do I crave for just that touch
when yours is more than enough
but you know I'm a woman and am longing for someone
to share my days and nights with, experience life with
Get married and have kids, but I'm losing patience
So if now is not the time then God,
please layer me with angels
to protect me when I'm feeling high...
Just turn off the rush, flowing through my blood
Just cover me, with yours
I can't take it anymore
Just hold me in your arms
and rock me fast to sleep
Just love this feeling out of me
Let me overdose on you
Be close, to you
Need you within me more than anything
but sometimes I'm still a fiend

for these fleshly things
Most days I'm fine but right now, I'm weak
Thank you God for keeping me
when so easily I could be
going right from withdrawal, to the real thing
Forgive me for every time I almost did
I know you hear my prayers for a husband
and if it wasn't for you I'd still be addicted
but instead, I'm in the process of recovering.

What the Lord Told Me

This morning the Lord told me
as I drove down, the lonely streets
"Your lonely days are numbered so rest in me."

I had to be sure that this was not 'me speak'
Turn down my Alicia Keys, so I could hear clearly
It was then I had certainty in these words
But what did they mean?

If my lonely days are numbered, well... by how many?
But the Lord, didn't provide me with a calendar
He just said, "Trust in me."

I thought about how odd it would be
for my husband to come into my life
when I'm struggling financially
Not exactly, where I'd planned to be
but then so far ahead, in ways
that God planned for me

I mean surely, he'd be forced to see me for me
at a time when, nothing is guaranteed
When I can't promise, the utmost stability
When rugs could be pulled, from beneath my feet
When I'm an artist full-time and very hungry

Some folks have hung me, like empty picture frames
no longer worthy of old memories
during the rough patches, they don't remember me
But then when everything is good again
or when they're in need...
Isn't it funny?

Like it's okay for them to burn your life story
in the fire place, between tongues of hate

when they see you in a weaker state
and feel as though they are playing it safe
that their sticks and stones will surely break...

I suppose by now most folks should know
Baby doll right here, is thick skinned
Although my heart, has gotten me in trouble
when I've given too much
Short changed myself
based on these receipts
printed from grief
when mascara dyed my pillow case
with eyelash calligraphy
and there, you have your ink
But see, it's running up

So there is no more need
for people to key punch
because I've unplugged the register
So from now on it is closed shop
on my being hurt

And I'd rather be lonely
then treated coldly
My real family knows me
although perfect we will never be
Making it through adversity
and being around people
who act abusively
are two different things

Sometimes it feels like,
some folks have abandoned me
But that is just Gods
protective hands on me

Steering me clear
of the wolves on these streets
Even if a life without wolves
seems lonely

Let's face the reality
Truly good hearts are a rarity
Something unique
Something you don't find
in everybody

So He hides me
Guards my purity
He knows my heart
has been through war
but that it didn't defeat me

God-serving women
don't fall easily
From now on,
the only place I'll fall
is to my knees
Living my life prayerfully
so I can listen to Him Speak

Oh Lord speak to me...
You know it's so lonely
climbing to the top
Sometimes I just think,
I need a man to come hold me
but still, I turn to God

I don't give into what my flesh wants
when I know that can get me in trouble
and that lifestyle, I had to stop

But oh how I miss, a warm pair of arms
How I miss a kiss, in the bottom of my heart
It's hard to repress this feeling
from swarming around me like sharks

but that's when the Lord said it again,
"Your lonely days are numbered,"
He says, "Don't let these things
get under, your skin,"
and Lord knows it's tempting
for a natural born morning time lover
to long for the skin, the skin of another

Especially when I'm hurting
from having to be alienated in
a world, of false mothers and brothers
False members
that call themselves blood,
but come like bad water
Polluted with toxic stuff
that I don't want in my cup

Overflowing with treasures
and gifts of all sorts
Blessings, endeavors
The Lord gives me more
When I ask Him
"What did I deserve this for?"
He says, for focusing on Him
in the eye of the storm

For walking on water
even when I felt,
like I was sinking before

For being stronger,
even when Satan
wants me more
than ever before
because I'm even
more valuable
then I was before...

But Devil,
my soul is kept
Better go back to hell
before you get hexed
In the name of Jesus!

Sure there are times when I've wept
Driving down these lonely streets
Wishing I had someone to caress
Take my softness easily
Don't be so hard on me
Don't forget I've still got it in me
I'm not just all sweet
Need somebody who isn't
foolish enough
to try to walk all over me

Lord I don't want to hurt nobody
But oh, people sure
be wanting to hurt me
Yes they do

And while I've chosen
to go down these lonely streets
only because it's where
you've called me to be

You know a woman's got needs
Yes she does
I'm not speaking sexually
just to clarify
While that may be
one element of me
I'm talking about,
being spiritually hungry for love
Beyond just emotions see
Beyond any chemical drug
I need love, Lord I need love

Have you ever needed love so much
that you felt like calling someone up
Just don't call the wrong one
Looking in your phone
at all of these numbers
Finger on the buttons
Ready to dial
until someone picks up

But before you call them
Ask yourself, is this a real friend?
Is this someone, on whom you can depend?
It hurts when the person you confide in
could care less about your problem
Too stuck on themselves
to reach out and help

You need someone who will say...
"Let's pray,"
not a man or woman who will say
"Let's lay,"

no see, you need someone
whose hands will lay in the right way
Someone who wants to take the pain away
Someone who loves you, every single day
Someone who goes through God
before a move is made
Someone who doesn't try to pay
for their sins, through your grace
Someone who isn't cheating on the Lord
with a lack of inward essence
Someone who doesn't
shake their dirt off on your slate
Someone who doesn't
try to burn off your face
leave you anonymous with no name

But when there is no one
Just call His name
I'm calling him
When the phone
leaves you hopeless
about to dial random digits
Just seek His face
I'm seeking

When you're driving
down these lonely streets
wishing you had some directions
Just ask Him to lead
I'm asking

Well if my lonely days are numbered
To God be the glory!!!
I believe I deserve to be happy
But Lord, please increase my capacity

to fuel me, on this journey
Lord, keep me company
when I'm lonely
Please comfort me
as I cross over into
unfamiliar territory.

AWAKENING

God Speak

Inside my heart of hearts, there is a paradise of love
Protected by the anointed guard of the creator above
So passionately, I longed to share it with everyone
but God has taught me a valuable lesson
of wearing our hearts on sleeves
Even if our own intentions are with positivity
There are those who are possessed
by demonic entities whom wish to deceive
There are those who will pretend to be friendly
just to ride on your coattail to that place you thrive to be
and there are those who continuously
talk cheap behind your back
For how can a poor spirit
see your spiritual richness when that they lack?

So I am weary, of letting in the riffraff's
They only wish to set me back, get me sad
I'd much rather lather in
God's constant splash of renewal
Best to refresh rather than digress
Never expect less than shipwreck
from those who are envious
yet express the opposite
during face to face encounters
One would think flakiness
were a drug prescribed over counters
The way people stay getting high
off of setting illusions to feel power
Let there be no confusion during God's hour
which is always now
When he calls on me to pray, I shall bow
Obediently accepting, what he asks of His child
Even when His way creates tension, we must obey
Seek His face, trying our best to remain fearless
Make decisions based on His way
even when we can't make sense of it
Time will clear it, God is never late
so we too shall come on time
to worship His undying faith
Thanking him, raising hands to the sky
Ask forgiveness for our mistakes
Pleading for him to maximize
Be not surprised,
when the capacity of God strips you of pride
Know that the old you must die,
in order for you to begin new
Old ways need to be left behind,
Whatever be required, abide
Even if it means loving your enemies
Praying for the very people who planted black seeds

in hope your growth would be attacked by the weeds
But those who sew, will also reap
so be not vengeful, in thought, nor deed
Believe that He will make you successful
in front of those not on His team
For spiritual warfare
comes with the territory of being kept
The bigger the battle there,
the closer you are to being blessed
You are His, body, mind, and spirit
Submit to him even when skies are clearest
When those rain clouds come again
to whom do you call?
So when the sun is still shining
to whom shall you fall?
Offer His love above all
Never to be misguided by your heart
Let God choose
to who shall receive the key to yours
as it belongs to Him
He knows who it's for
Be blind in all but His vision
and you will live the life you were destined for
before you were first born
Now be born again
God said only faithful servants
will inherit the kingdom.

One Prayer Too Short

What if you were one prayer too short?
Just one praise too small
What if all He wanted
was for you to sing His song?
What if your deliverance was
in the passion of your heart?
Would the screaming and shouting get you far
if deep down you weren't a believer at all?
You're so close but so far
Too busy just being a churchgoer
to be a true worshiper
This isn't just a Sunday job
God's shift is round' the clock
What if he gave you what you want,
would you give him what he needs?
If the only time you call is
when asking him to do you deed
then when he doesn't respond,
do you act surprisingly?
Now there may be
just a mustard seed of faith inside of me
but I'm nurturing that seed to grow
So before you begin to think
you are more high than me
ask yourself
if you're just putting on a holy show
When you go home, and you're all alone
Do you still put him first?
Do you go right back to selling soul
or are you letting God work?
Are you making any effort to make a change
If you don't know about the flesh and spirit battle,
it isn't because you're a saint
Maybe it's because
you're sitting in the same place

as you were yesterday
See at least if I slip,
I can still say I'm on the wheel
Instead of pretending to be perfect
to the point where I can't heal
What I consider slipping now
would have been me climbing not long ago
But see I'm constantly building inside of my temple
I'm quite capable of being critical all by myself
Know when I'm going wrong, woman enough to say it
But if I give it all to God, He said he will take it
We can't lie to the creator about our situations
He knows about our fornication
He knows about our drug addictions
Idol worshiping, adultery,
like whom are we kidding?
He knows if the baby isn’t his
He knows about your unfaithful relationships
There is no hiding it from him
But we've all been guilty of trying
See I'd rather be real
Give him something He can feel
Rather than come one prayer too short
Just one praise too small
What if all He wanted
was for you to sing His song?
What if your deliverance
was on the tip of your tongue?
Would you thank Him for
all the things He's done
Would you walk with Him to freedom
or choose to stay stuck?
Would you be too busy
hating on your neighbor
with her hair done better than yours

to pay attention when God speaks into your core
Fellas, would you be too busy flexing
for the women to receive a word?
At the end of the day your suits and ties
aren't nothing but suits and ties
If you don't have Jesus,
who cares about what you can buy
God has a blessing tailored just for you
He doesn't care if
you've got on some new shoes
when you are still one prayer too short
Just one praise too small
What if all He wanted
was for you to sing His song?
Would His promise of forgiveness
for the things you did wrong
mean anything at all?
See He knows we're all sinners
in both our actions and thoughts
but he wants us to prove to Him
that we are down for His walk
when none of us can afford to be
one prayer too short.

Finding Me

So many questions...
I wish I had all the answers
but the truth is I'm at that fork in the road
That strange place where there is no sign
telling you which way to go
yet a urgency to make a choice
as the hour glass is tipped
Trying to get through to God's voice
Get rid of all this static
It's like a migraine in my soul
Blinding me while I'm trying to find in me
the courage to let go of all the fears
that make me indecisive when I know
that now isn't the moment
to be letting seconds slip away
Could it be as simple as finding
the right words to write this poem
or as natural as the gift
that springs from these flows?
But it feels kind of like
having a writer's block on my goals
Like I'm spinning in circles
yet still seeking growth
and everybody wants to know,
"Ms. Tabu, when is the next show?"
"When is the book or album release?"
Why I'm missing in action
on my dreams lately
Maybe I'm just finding me
or maybe I'm digging too deep
But I know one thing with certainty
My passion for poetry is here always
No matter how these seasons change
No matter how many logical reasons surface
Like..."It just don't pay!"

I refuse to believe God plants seeds accidentally
All of this confusion must be the enemy
blocking me from my blessing
Manipulating what God promised me
but it's time for me to believe
No weapon formed against me shall prosper
However far off the trail I think I've wandered
My destiny has been written
Look at my haters smiling
off of the mere thought that I'm defeated
and those who love me are
just wondering where I've been
I'm surviving spiritual attacks and depression
but apparently I'm still breathing
Just needed a reminder
I've been through worse things
Satan is just a liar still mocking the king
Got me praying in my sleep
Feeling negative energies
trying to leach onto me subconsciously
while in my most vulnerable state
Waking up to my own voice
saying "In Jesus' Name!"
Thinking I'm going crazy
but really I'm going sane
Thinking that I was lost
when really, I've been saved
My flesh is longing for the old legs
while learning how to walk my new way
I'm kneeling down to pray
before I even make a move
This is more than another page,
this is the rebirth of Tabu.

My Mind

Open, but never loose
Sometimes mistaken for being closed
but truly just firm in core values
Not able to be man ruled
Knows when to choose
By only one God, fueled
Seeks truth,
reads between lines
Sees lies, doesn't believe things
just because others do
Analyzes, no time for the mindless
Digs for treasures, drops jewels
never carelessly
Travels places others don't dare to see
Loaded with weapons of mass destruction
Targeting ignorance, they never saw it coming
Assigned to a hit list of souls to save
Bring death to the old ways
Breathe new into people
My mind, plays in the dirt,
does the work, wears the vest,
so the bullets back don't hurt
when attacked with words by nonbelievers
My mind, knows the power of tongue
is among the greatest
Controls its thoughts
when they become too dangerous
so that what is said is spiritually equipped
with God and not just it
Load the mental clip with Jesus
Send everything else to perish
Sometimes my mind has to
put me on its own hit list
to die in the flesh daily
and then begin to live

Sometimes my mind moves faster
then the pain within that burns slow
but remembers what I'm after
and reminds me of my goals
My mind translates my purpose
from the Lord's lips to my will within
as though I'm just the middle person
in this communication
As my heart signs the agreement,
my mind reads the fine print
and my spirit tells my flesh,
it is time to be obedient
My mind, hands itself over to Him
and God says,
"Let me do the thinking,
you just make the moves.
Don't forget I'm always with you
even when the enemy tries to
send you out of tune.
Open your eyes my child,
the wheel is still here.
I've kept you on it through every trial,
even through your worldly fears.
Rebuke all that is not of me,
for you will prove that you love me
when you begin to trust me.
Yes it is then when your mind,
will set you free
and this I know,
because your mind belongs to me,
the creator of all things,
including the freewill
with which you chose me."

I Am Pure

I wrote this poem for the Lord, Jesus Christ, my Savior
I wanted to tell Him, thank you for making me pure
I hear people laughing at me right now
They are too ignorantly happy, to push away the clouds
Not clouds like in the sky, closer to heaven than us
But clouds of pollution, of poison, and dust
and not dust like the kind, God rose man from
But the kind, that will mess your whole system up
But I wrote this poem, to pull every plug
I pulled the plug, on their lies...
I pulled the plug, on their disguise
I pulled the plug, on the demons
I pulled the plug, on the men
who are after my life
I pulled the plug on the flashbacks
of the times I was victimized
I turned off the flashlight in my mind
and let my new eyes, begin to shine

It was a worthy sacrifice
For a man who doesn't hurt me,
named Jesus Christ
A man who cleansed all of my impurities
then called me divine
Smiled upon me
and said, you are mine
He walks with me by His side
He's proud to have me all the time
The only time He tells me to hide
is when He's hiding with me
Protecting me
He says daughter, confide in me
Correcting me but never beheading me
He handles me affectionately
Teaches me an intimacy that isn't sexually

And in my deepest confessions,
He still loves me, unconditionally

Lord, I wrote this poem to tell you I'm sorry
I'm sorry for my moments of disobedience
I'm sorry for not being, more scholarly in my reading
I'm sorry for the times when I didn't know
if I was coming or leaving
For my secrecies that defeated me
When you just need to hear me speak...
I'm sorry for my issues with forgiveness
I'm sorry for when I only committed to you
with one foot in...
But thank you, for your goodness
during times of sin
I changed because you kept pushing
when I couldn't
I couldn't do it alone anymore
I couldn't live the same anymore
I had to either come in the way
or leave and close the door
So I wrote this poem to say I am yours
Pure, sweet, pretty, heavenly
Wings growing beautifully
Honing gifts of poetry
Only through the God who hones me

When people,
tried to ho me
Abuse me, use me, dirty me
Exclude me, isolate me
Confuse me, drug me
Make me unruly
Tempt me, to being angry
Distract me, lose my sanity

Strip me, of my inner peace
Ban me, behind the scenes
Pimp me, and my poetry
Impregnate me, to control me
Lie to me, through their teeth
Cheat on a queen of monogamy
Peeve and bother me
Stoop me to living dishonorably
Spread rumors,
make sure no one wanted me
Alienate and abandon me
Raped and molested me
Pretend to relate but lesser me
Heart break and never treasure me
Dig my grave at the same time
as they pretend to pleasure me
Pervert and de-feathered me
Hurt and wound me consecutively
with no room to even breathe
Before other wolves follow
in their lead, attempting to
deceive God's sheep

See, I wrote this poem to speak
To lift my voice, to bleed out my humanity
To let the Lord hear my heartbeat
To tell Him, that he can call on me...
When he needs me for delivery
When he needs me for my literacy
My gift of expression, linguistically
On my knees, or on my feet
Wake me up out of my sleep
In the church, or in the streets
The homeless, the prostitutes,
or the rebellious teens

The forgotten about
The looked over
The projects, where the ghettos be
The roses growing between concrete
Oh Lord, wherever you want me to be
You are my best friend, lover, and brother to me
You are the only one, who could heal me
You dug deep, into the dirt
where you removed these weeds
and this hurt, this grief, the agony of being deceived
Remove the ability to ignore things I feel intuitively
Yes you restored me, re-sensitized me
You never ever, ever denied me
But rather, filled me with seeds of glory
You support me, you adore me
You have nurtured me, to spiritual maturity
Yes, you, have cured me
of emotional mental, spiritual, psychological, disease
from the things, that were done to me

See Lord, I wrote this poem
to tell you I'm ready
to increase, my loyalty
Look at all the ways, He spoils me
All these gifts, surely can't be for me
What did I do to ever deserve this?
I've never for a day in my life been perfect
I bet you there are a few times,
I've even cursed Him
When I was angry at
the same men who hurt Him
See I bet you there are times
that I was churchless
Because I wasn't trying
to hear His Word, yet

Oh God,
there were many nights
I've fornicated
when I should have waited
My life could have been more painless
If I had only listened to men a little less
See I bet you that in all my emptiness
In all my, stress
In all my mess
That the Lord knew I was anointed
and so very blessed
by the merciful Father, of the Godhead
So I wrote this poem
to tell the Lord yes all over again
A renewal of vows
There is no way, and no how
I could have made it out without
I know that now
Didn't know it then
But here at this, holy gathering
between me and the son of salvation
I am professing without embarrassment
That I love Him even if they hate him
I put no one above Him
No one can take Him
I claim Him, he's mine for life
I'm more than a maiden
More than a future wife
My hand was first taken, by Jesus Christ
And oh, some people they call me crazy
Asking why I wear this ring of purity
when I haven't been a virgin in a long time
But in the Lord's eyes,
I'm purified from the inside out
In the Lord's eyes,

I've been redesigned,
I'm better now
Never said I was perfect,
but I am purer than I was in my past life
So you can laugh, that's alright

But I can't bring you to heaven with me
We each have our time to go
So if you think anybody can reserve a seat
This isn't the movies and there are no tickets sold
You've got to earn this, from the Holy Ghost
It doesn't come from your money
It doesn't come from your clothes
It doesn't come from a world of materials
Salvation is the way to save souls
but sanctification is the only way
to get through those gates that stay closed
They don't just open, for any old Joe or Jane doe
Claiming they believe, now that they know
You should have known
what the consequences were
for choosing to live for your flesh
when the flesh is impure
Should have known, based on the word
that getting to heaven,
requires more than going to church
Should have known when it was all a blur
that only in His name could things get clearer
Now I may not be all the way there
But the Lord knows I care
don't want to sit in Hell's electric chair
Don't want to live a life of sin, so unfair
when Jesus was crucified on the cross
when he was pained, by all of our
sinful ways, actions, thoughts

all at once before his Father
As the people watched, the Son of God die
in assumption that he'd never rise
If it were up to them,
there would be no Jesus Christ

But God purifies
Exceeds expectations
to shock our eyes into believing
and yet, still we betray Him
You're leaving, I'm staying
You're busy huffing and heaving
while I'm busy praying
I have freedom, you have enslavement
I serve the kingdom
and you are Satan's to play with
I'm filled with love, not hatred
I'm covered in the blood and not tainted
I'm only pure because God taketh
I'm only sure because I'm a witness
of something they say we can't see,
touch, or taste it
But even if that were true
and we stick with the basics
We can feel! Do you feel it?
How will you heal if you conceal it
Give it to Him, all of your dirt
He will make you pure if you put Him first
and then you will be lifted of every curse
as you begin to acknowledge
what in Him you are worth
and forever be purer
then you once were.

Spiritual Warfare

It lingers in your flesh,
waiting for the perfect moment
to penetrate through your weakness
at a time when you need to be strongest
Tugging at your mind, body, and spirit
Voices in your head, to the point where
you are deaf to hearing the things God said
Now you're misled, trouble steering
Don't know which direction to turn in
Heart is hurting, feeling worthless
Searching for a way to purge this
Vision is blurring, but the world it keeps turning
Desperate for a second to get it together
Could you put yourself back in check,
if something could ease the pressure
Now you're being tempted by lustful pleasures
Jezebel's spirit must be after your soul
We've all been down that road
when whichever way we go,
it seems to be trouble
The angel's presence is felt, but too subtle
If you had a mustard seed of faith, could it grow?
If you had a dream to chase, could you create a goal?
But nothing even matters anymore
when you're on the battle lines
as the enemy attacks you from inside
Don't know which decision is right
Curl up and die or live your life
It's hard to live when your spirit
has been stabbed with knives
and demons leech on to your pride
It hurts too much to cry,
but you lie that you're alright
Who could even pray
if you display that you're okay?

Then suddenly you hear a voice say,
"Don't let another moment slip away,
don't let the Devil win today,
by falling prey to spiritual warfare,
seek my face and I'll be there."
In comatose by a deep stillness,
where words the Lord spoke bring healing
Finally you can hear him without all the noise
Just turn to the light and darkness be gone
There is no safer place than God's arms in the storm.

Spirit of Forgiveness

For so long I couldn't forgive you,
but I couldn't even forgive me
After all, I have to take partial responsibility
for the things I let you do to me
For the time and the energy
consumed by being around you
For being, mistreated and abused
And it's sad to say
that new victims come a dime a dozen
But I'm just glad to say
when I left there was still something
A little shine left inside of me
Even if it took physical lines being crossed
Progressing from the psychological brainwash
to grabbing me some kind of way
Yes I thank God I walked away
And while I've labeled you
one of my biggest mistakes
There's something I have to say
I really hope you change
Think I've found the strength to pray
even for those who have wronged me
I hope there comes a day when you go get saved
and repent for all the women
you have hurt even before me
While I still would rather not see your face
or wind up at the same place
and have no desire for a hand shake
or fellowship in any kind of way
I've let go of all the hate
and the bondage that still kept me in that cage
My heart was singing the same sad song
but I told you butterflies don't belong in glass jars
So if you ever thought for a second
that you would stop me from success then,

you're in for a great surprise
You never won my soul, just wounded my pride
I'm so thankful that I'm not living in your lies
Can't even believe I was that woman
It all seems so long ago
Regardless of the fact that
you found me when I was vulnerable
It still trips my mind to rewind
but I can't remember the last time I cried over you
Still if I had one last thing to say, I'd say thank you
because it took being used and abused one last time
before I finally gave my life to Christ
So I guess you served your purpose in my life
but I won’t play the bag lady for you
so I'm, cutting off the last of these soul ties
by forgiving and leaving the past behind
Yes, the spirit of forgiveness has become one with mine.

Tranquil Storm

Here I am in stillness
Darkness, ego outage
Tranquility began to rain on my spirit
as I pushed aside the blinds and watched
from the outside looking in
Observing the beauty of peace
in its natural state
I thought to myself,
I'd really love to be that way
every day, just sound
Enveloped by serenity
Without superficial dependencies
substituting for empty, pretending we are okay
But the reality is, sometimes I'm not okay
Sometimes I could burst into tears right there
Yet I restrain, for fear of
having to explain what's wrong
Waiting for that moment
when I don't have to be strong
Does it ever come?
Still holding on by threads
Finally, silence...
All is quiet but the downpour within
You may need an umbrella
if you choose to come in
But please have no confusion
For these storms are not angry storms,
they are storms of passion
If you shall dare be drenched in them,
know that you will soon be anointed in love
Do not mind the strikes of lightening
I do apologize if they seem frightening
but it has all been bottled in for too long
So please do not be bothered
by this tranquil storm within my heart.

The Truth

There are some days I wake up,
not knowing how on earth
I'll make it through now
There are still those moments,
when I'm feeling so down and out
and sometimes I reminisce on a few things I did
Wishing I never dated him or thinking of things
I'd have done different if I could rewind back
But then I think about
the lack of testimony I would have
I accept the fact that I went through it
so that someone won't have to
or so that when they do, I can pull them through
to salvation on the other side
See, there are still tears that fall from my eyes
and there are still nights when
it feels like I'm just dying inside
Asking God where I'm headed with my life
Am I on the wheel or am I just
delusional with what I feel
But when I feel him speak to me,
I know I'm where I'm meant to be
Even if it doesn't all make sense to me
See I'm not really the type of woman
who pretends to be someone other than me
But sometimes there is still pain behind my smile
Sometimes I don't know whose number to dial
I'm thankful for that one real friend
on the other end of the line
who won't spill out my secrets
when I'm going through a predicament
and just need to vent
Won't judge me if I cuss a bit or show weakness
Instead that friend reassures me of my strength
so that I don't forget the gifts with which I'm blessed

The truth is, I haven't even started living yet
I'm just learning how to walk with God
Growing up without guidance
sped up the process of being grown
to the point where I missed out
on some parts of spiritual growth
So I've been doing a lot of searching in my soul
while experiencing deliverance
from those girl years stole
Now I'm a woman just trying to be whole
Still there are times I feel less than half
Like I'm just not successful enough
for the expectations I had
But then I realize that's the whole problem
Me trying to play the role of God again
So I step aside from my flesh,
inviting the Holy Spirit inside
Covered in anointing oil,
crying "Lord, I can't take it no more!"
Let it all out until the hurt is gone
All my life I've had to be strong
but right now I just want to be healed
I said right now, I'm keeping it real
This is the truth being revealed
so don't get it twisted
Just because I'm saved doesn't mean
stormy weather don't visit
But it does mean that I'll be carried through
Survive things that might seem impossible
Yes it's true sometimes I don't pick up the phone
cause' I'm feeling so emotional
Not that I want to be alone
Just that I want to hear the Lord
Man's advice is only human so
I turn to the only truth I really know

Asking God to help me be successful
in all the ways He intended for
I don't want my talents to be wasted
I want them used for the purpose
that I was put here to serve, Lord
Whatever he asks of me I'll do
and right now he's just asking for the truth.

Feed the Poor

Rich poor folks and poor rich folks
Digging for material riches to become whole
Empty stomachs full and full stomachs empty
For it is the man with a full soul
who has been fed properly
Break past the social conditioning
I had The Word for breakfast
to speed up my deliverance
My metabolism can wait
This cleansing process makes change
You can't put this in a cup,
but it will overflow in His name
Some folks see your strength as a weakness
while they are busy reading books like
"Men Are from Mars, Women Are from Venus,"
trying to understand each other
with no foundation for relationships
How about trusting the hands that created this
earth and every living thing existing in it
Stop gaining useless knowledge just to feel empowered
Forget the Mayan Calendar and astrology books
Celebrity news and Cosmopolitan looks
Rappers who dis their savior just to record push,
to millions of unsaved people in the universe.

The Seed Harvester

Her 'off' days bring more fruition than 'on' ones
A chance to tend to the seeds full of promise
while planting new possibilities
She would like the masses to think she's being lazy
while she nurtures future miracles beneath her feet
She walks the grounds with roots that run deep
When she comes around,
brothers discover the scent of a queen
Inhaling her healing energies
Anointed by maternal instincts
Always ready to birth life into empty heart beats,
She's much more than what she seems
She breathes humbly, so not to suffocate her dreams
Trails of love she leaves wherever she be
Soft whispers from her soul speak, "Follow me,"
she leads, for those who need to be taught, she teach
For those who are lost, to salvation she brings
To hearts in need of a song, she sings
She does all of these things and asks for nothing
For she believes faithfully that she has everything
Even when her circumstances would have many running
She be still, in the eye of the storm
Awaiting the spirit to fill her with His downpour
Rain on her spirit, flood her with fertility
until new beginnings spring from within
She remains pure even when the enemy bathes her in sin
She offers forgiveness when they don't deserve it
Chooses her battles wisely when the war isn't worth it
She is far from perfect but she is perfecting
Through the power of words, she offers direction
She is the subject so often mentioned
by those who would wish
to leave ashes on her reflection
Still she marks the intersection
where her crossover begins

Listening for when
Prepared for obedience
Continuously harvesting,
for she knows it's her season
Submitting to the process of bringing and leaving
Allowing room for the weeding by most divine hands
while speaking her destiny into existence, “Prosperity!"
She says it again until she is certain it has been activated
Although she understands this journey won't be painless
She bleeds the blood of a legend and accepts the territory
But for the fruit of her harvest, she gives God all the glory.

SURRENDER

Ready for New

This feeling of discomfort keeps coming over me
Clearly the expiration date on this situation
has come and left many times
But it's like I'm stuck in this
predicament in the physical
and then become a prisoner of my mind
How can I change everything in my life
to fit the new woman I've become?
It feels like a pair of shoes that just don't fit
but you keep wearing them due to your circumstances
There is nothing like some fresh kicks
Feel like I'm living at a new address
but dealing with the same old 'ish'
This depression should have been done with
but I'm so frustrated, tired of this ghetto life
Longing for finer things, tired of being alone
Want a man to truly love me

Sick of being confused, not knowing what to do
No better way to explain this than "Ready for New"
Wanting my own crib,
and for my career to get started
Lord please send me a husband
to hold me down when I can't do it solo
and the only place I feel at ease,
is on the microphone
I think it'd be really nice
to come home to a man who knows
just how to calm the storm in my soul
when everything seems to be
spinning out of control
and I want to believe in my dreams
but sometimes I don't know
where I'm really going to be
by the time I'm thirty years old
How am I going to meet these goals?
Progress seems to be going so slow
but time seems to be going too fast
while going through this process
of healing from the past
I'm ready for the new life I never got to have
but first I've got to find my own path
Honestly this business degree
has me with second thoughts
I really need stability,
don't want to struggle like my pops
Working all those jobs
just to stay in the same debt
I wish these talents would pay off
Maybe if I get more motivated
See I'm not disregarding my part
Responsibility I must take
I'm just speaking my heart

but I know I've made mistakes
Either way it don't change the way I feel
when I'm so ready for new
but riding on these old wheels
So ready for new but got the same bills
So ready for new but living in the same crib
while my spirit has moved to a different location
waiting for the rest of me to catch up
I'm ready for new, forget the old stuff
Old love, old clothes, old train of thought
I want a chance to be successful
while I'm still young
I'm ready for new and so done
cleaning this old mess up
Ready for new and I'm not giving up
Got to shed this old skin off
Been procrastinating one minute too long
Ready for my new clock, forget the time
I just want the hands of God in my life.

A Prayer Poem

Can you imagine what I'm feeling
on a rainy day all alone?
Starting to feel
the woman in me take control
No longer numb to the pain,
now I'm letting go
While this process has been slow
It hasn't been easy, please believe me
It has been a lot of confusion at times
when the enemy wants to deceive me
There has been some resistance, but I know
part of my duty in Christ is forgiveness
I know it's just one life in this flesh that I'm living
but there have been too many days,
I've watched just slip away
while going through this phase,
this emotional state
Caught me in a funny place
like I was sleeping but now I'm awake
and Lord there's twice the work to do
But I know if it's on my plate then I am able to
because God said he won't give me
more than I can handle
So I'm putting my war gear on
Getting ready to take all of my fears on
To tell you the truth I'm so sick of me
just turning my back on my dreams
Not living up to my full potential
Letting the enemy mess with my soul
Distracting me from my goals
In Jesus' name, I command you to go!!!
There is no reason to be on this road
when I see clearly the way to freedom
Tired of promising myself things
if I'm not going to keep them

Like tomorrow it will change,
I'll get it right this time
No! The time is today!
This moment is mine
I want to be able to say,
I'm doing just fine
and really mean it next time
My past I want leave it behind
My heart I want to save for a man
who will love me for life
So here I am, can you see me now?
These are the things I am feeling deep down
Maybe through my transparency,
I can help someone else
Lord please carry me,
you know I need some help
Just that extra push when I feel like giving up
Just that reminder that by you I am Loved
Lord please just get me over this hump
It's time to move forward
Let all of my old ways be done!

Just Tuck Me In

Please come tuck me in tonight
Nobody else ever does it right
Turn off all the lights so I can see
something that shines brighter than electricity
A power that will stay on eternally
You make my insides look like the city
while gazing down from a balcony
Like finally, I've become somebody
out here in this cold world
So many dogs,
trying to trample my pearls
Sometimes I want to hide
But even the covers, don't keep me safe
when I'm missing you like a lover
that has gone so far away
And it's so hard to cry,
when the tears come like quicksand
pulling down my mind until I'm sinking again
Wishing for a moment to be
intimate with your spirit like never before
For the first time I'm desperate,
never wanted anyone more
You know I'm sensitive
when I'm already sore
from the pain that's been
messing with old wounds
and I'm feeling torn
Needing your affection
to soothe each layer of my core
I want to feel you deeply,
don't you hear me Lord?
Am I speaking in your tongue
My heart is still beating
off of the last time I felt your hymn
But you mustn't be so silent this time

While your angelic violins sound divine
I need a downpour for the strength to fight
You promised me you'd be by my side
I'll be still until you save me from destructing
Awaiting patiently for you to tuck me in
I know I haven't been abandoned,
but the Devil is a liar!
I just need the comfort of your hands
to lift me higher
I'm sorry for sounding so expired
I'm truly trying to build your empire
Lord I'm just so tired of only getting by
Holding on by this golden string
tied into my heart like a harp
with key parts missing
I'm just wishing they'd return
so I could sing again
But then I am faithful
that you have a bigger plan
So I'm willing and able
to learn how to withstand
But tonight Lord,
I just need you to come and tuck me in
then rock me like a child
until I'm innocent again.

Say Yes

So many days I've spent alone
Many folks would go insane
but I was searching for my soul
Found it on the road to salvation
I saw the places I've been along the way
Even fantasized about some old sins
In fact, I almost slipped into some traps
but He kept me… "Who?" you ask
That's a funny question people always have
but answer them and funny they act
A friend and I had this discussion about that
How you can say God but don't mention the cross!
About Jesus Christ, nobody wants to talk.
Could it be they are scared of the thought
that there is heaven and hell after all?
That there is prosecution beyond the courts
for the things you do wrong?
Could it be that the imagery of
nails through His wrists is, much too graphic?
Maybe it's denial of the Biblical passage
They say man wrote it so it isn't true
But they believe in science's excuse
for how we came to be
Some religiously believe in Astrology
but the galaxy, stars, & moon,
God created that too
So who are these 'gods' you be praying to?
The Devil has many faces
Pagans and Atheists are among Satan's
favorite puppets to play with
Manipulating you that Jesus doesn't exist
You're just being tricked, soul being pimped
How can you be forgiven for sins if you deny Him?
Do you ever wonder what if you are badly mistaken?
Never too late for changing if you're still alive

But know that you can die anytime
If you think it's all brainwash
please tell me, who made us?
Oh, now we drawing blanks cause',
you can't think of one reasonable explanation
You just want to live your life the same way
Living for Him is a threat to
the worldly things you like to do
Don't want any Godly rules
In short, you enjoy being Satan's prostitute
Conditioned that it's freedom in that prison
Nothing seems off limits
Lust is glorified, and it fits like a glove
Just want the high and your friends say its right
so anyone who tells you otherwise is against you
Tell me when did Jesus become the enemy?
Tell me why you are breathing
when you don't deserve to be?
How many chances do you need?
Are your pleasures on earth worth pain eternally?
You call me crazy but when it's your time,
you'll wish you changed your mind
Funny how even those who don't believe it
so often call His name when they need it
Suddenly you're on your deathbed
and your last resort is Jesus
So I ask you again,
how many chances does it take?
Are you too hard headed to be saved?
My friend, for you... I pray.

When God Calls

When God calls, I will answer,
He always does for me
I will divert my attention
away from whatever I'm doing
Shifting my focus to Him
Ignoring Him doesn't work anyway
Trust me, I've tried more than a few times
Better off following His will
even if it means offending others
Even if you have to excuse yourself
from the table to take that call
Even if they talk about you
How you done changed
Been acting strange
Harder to reach than you used to be
Sometimes, we need to be less available
Meditate on The Word a little
Even if the solitude drives folks up the wall
"I've been texting, I've been calling,"... Chill!
Tell them, I've been busy listening to Him
Only the wrong folks could be offended by that
Don't sweat losing people who pose as friends
Real friends try to understand what you're going through
They don't smear your name soon as you're on a hiatus
Real friends don't change up from lovers to haters
Remember that when folks who were close
those you trusted most, hurt you bad
or judge you for any microscopic flaw
as soon as you got saved
Gave your life to the Lord
so they assumed you'd never sin no more
like humanity isn't in your skin no more
See this here is a spiritual war
People will try to pull you back
They will prey on the weakness

they knew you used to have
Be ready, be weary
Prepare yourself for the test
When God calls,
clear your head of the mess
Whatever you're feeling
Wherever you're at then
Despite the distractions
You must answer to Him
For He has a message
to reveal a higher purpose in your life
Be mindful of that fact when
you leave God hanging on the line
but then expect Him to answer
always, on your time.

Step Out of the Comfort Zone

What do we do when the comfort zone, is stunting growth?
When we get so comfortable, in what we used to know
that we get lost in a cycle of doing what we're used to, so
We make old out of new homes
We flirt with old roads
We take the back way just to go back astray
Just to come back to say, something must change
Then we turn our backs to the brightly lit pathway
And we, distract the past away instead of living today
Articulately form new habits to bandage our issues away
Self-inflicted pain on our missions misplaced
When it comes time to blood trace,
we wonder why we're missing the vein
Too blind to see, we're living in vain
Then cross streets like blind men without white canes
with no higher senses to lead us there safe
We fly skies like birds senseless
with broken wings that don't pray
We dream with eyes that don't open in time to be saved
Then press rewind on those moments we let slip away
Forever forgetful that it's never too late
See our being resentful of the damage we make
is often our biggest mistake
When the bough breaks that cradled our fate
We seek to pacify pride instead of seeking God's face
Grown in size but like babies behaved
Trading our yeses for maybes that don't make us wait
Impatience misleads us to a brothel of hate
So do we choose to be slaves to a life bounded by chains?
Do we want more but refuse to be raised?
Settling for this minimum wage
What do we promote in this age
but love sold at the expense of being lustful?
When did love become so replaceable
with things of no value traceable?

When did the sunrise
stop reminding people of The Son's rise
On the tips of our tongues do we
speak Jesus Christ with hearts made of guns
that shoot down His fight to breathe us new life?
Do we take flight every time God tries
to speak truth through our lies?
Too weak to die in the flesh, so we just get by
Searching for a stronger lung to survive
Hurting a little longer when comes the night
as lonely pillows remind us of
the comfort zones that confined us
Couldn't make our minds up
so we accept being in the minus
Depositing ourselves in all the wrong places
We ask God for help but then we don't take it
Pretenders of being complacent while tortured by Satan
We don't know the hour but we still waste it
While going insane in a mental bath we can't bathe in
If the filth is not draining, we're only decaying
But our ride is still waiting, please don't miss it again
This is our way in to get out of this still painting
that never seems to move us to move up
To choose true love over the comfort zone
True love, the kind that won't vote us off the boat
then drown us in our misery until we're miserable
and no longer know, the difference between
standing idle and serving the purpose God wrote
We can make it work if we push when comfort pulls
At the ends of our break through, we will begin to grow
Our glasses once half-empty will finally overflow
Deep down we know, it is time to step out of the comfort zone.

ABOUT THE AUTHOR

Born in Connecticut, Tabitha Marie Long, better known on stage as Ms. Tabu, is a well-rounded writer and performance poet, writing her first poem at the young age of ten. She then discovered a new gift for rhythm and lyricism at thirteen and has been songwriting ever since. Not to mention her theatrical roots that stem from early childhood and have grown around her wordplay and envelop her artistic demeanor on stage.

For the audience, witnessing the real life inspired acts of Ms. Tabu can be like watching a clip from a dramatically enchanting play. In some of her writings, she focuses on interracial issues with pieces such as "I'm Not Worth Your Stereotypes," as she passionately promotes diversity through her nicely seasoned delivery of words. Both in and out of her artistry, Ms. Tabu is a humanitarian who advocates for social justice and equal rights. From her viewpoint, it is through her honesty and courageousness that others can be reached.

Extremely versatile, she also writes of many other subjects, such as ones pertaining to love, spirituality, and family. She takes lovers of her craft into her world to share her heart with them. Her work echoes of a soul being delivered from personal struggles, as she heals through each page of her life. She is both hip-hop and soulful with a touch of a woman's manifesto and a Free Verse style that lets her navigate from poetry to lyricism, making her a phenomenal performer.

Ms. Tabu has been featured at countless events and venues, mainly between Connecticut and New York City. On September 23rd 2010, Ms. Tabu successfully presented the grand debut of her show, "MIC2SOUL," which showcased new artists on a monthly basis.

A woman of many goals, Ms. Tabu is currently in the process of publishing her second poetry book, *Inkwells of Love*. She also has plans to record several Spoken Word albums based on the material in her books.

It would be easy for someone to assume that a person so artistically equipped would lack humility, but Ms. Tabu humbly perceives herself as a vessel with a purpose to deliver messages through her craft. She is on a God-given mission not only to give voice to the voiceless, but to instill healing and growth in people through relating experiences.

Thank you for reading Cross Points: The Poetic Diary of Ms. Tabu! I hope you've been blessed by the words I've shared.

Connect with me on my Facebook fan page at www.facebook.com/MsTabu, visit my website at www.MsTabu.com, or follow me on Twitter @OfficialMsTabu to stay informed on upcoming appearances, book signings, and the release of my second publication, *Inkwells of Love*.

41819564R00131

Made in the USA
Charleston, SC
12 May 2015